Face

A dialogue with Jesus

Lloyd Gardner

Pamela & Glenn,

It was indeed a pleasure to meet you at the Olallieberry Inn. It was certainly a meeting ordained by God. We hope the book blesses you by revealing how real and personal Jesus is. May we all meet & fellowship with Him face to face. God bless.

Lloyd & Mary

Eliezer Call Ministries

Face to Face a Dialogue with Jesus. Copyright © 2009 by Lloyd Gardner. All rights reserved. Printed in the United States of America. Permission to reproduce or transmit any form of this material will be granted with permission from Lloyd Gardner. Please contact Lloyd Gardner at mlgardner@netptc.net.

Unless otherwise indicated, all scripture quotations are the personal translation of the author.

Visit our website at http://eliezercall.com/

FIRST EDITION

† Acknowledgements

    I dedicate this book to Jesus and to all who desire to make Him the guest of honor in their lives. He wants to sit down with us and speak to us face to face about our lives. His presence and His simple but profound words will change even the most obstinate person. This book is dedicated to those who desire to leave the stilted, confines of religion and enter a loving relationship with the Lord.

    I extend a special thank you to all who stood with me during my cancer ordeal. You loved me and proved that love with your actions and I will never forget any of you. Foremost among these people is my precious wife Mary who was a strong, courageous caregiver when I was weak. I am continually falling deeper in love with her. A special thanks to my faithful children Matthew and Karis and their spouses Sylvia and Jim. I love you all.

    Many members of the body of Christ helped edit this book and give helpful suggestions. This is not a book completed by literary experts but one compiled and edited by the Holy Spirit through His people. Thank you all for your help.

    I wish for all who read this book a simple, real, living relationship with the Lord Jesus. God bless all who read. To Timm and B.J., John and Geri, the Monterey and Tollhouse saints and the many others who listened with open hearts—God bless you all.

† Contents

	Introduction: An Invitation to Enter His Presence	5
1	How it all Began	8
2	My Journey to the Judgment Seat	13
3	My Destiny	17
4	My Childhood Years	21
5	Joining the Family of God	25
6	Becoming a Follower of Christ	28
7	A Time of Rebellion	32
8	Into the Wilderness	36
9	God Clarifies His Purpose	42
10	Hints of Victory	45
11	The Collapse of America	48
12	The Rising up of the Church	57
13	I Will Build My Church	63
14	A New Wineskin	68
15	Drifting Away from Simplicity	74
16	Love: The Manifestation of God	78
17	The Mystery of Suffering	81
18	Forgiveness	89
19	Entering God's Rest	93
20	Finances in the Kingdom	99
21	Worship	105
22	Mary	110
23	Prayer	116
24	The Physical Appearance of Jesus	121
25	Becoming a Bondservant of the Lord	125
26	Divine Healing	128
27	My Commission: Tear down that wall	136
28	The Condition of the Organized Church	141
29	The Bride of Christ	154
30	The Gathering of the Champions	159
	Conclusion: How then should we Live?	163

† Introduction: An Invitation to Enter His Presence

As I have written this book I have been fighting a devastating battle against cancer. Non-Hodgkin's lymphoma invaded my body and robbed me of over fifty pounds and all of my bodily strength. I was physically devastated by various side effects of the chemo-therapy treatment. This challenge had the potential of having a very depressing affect on my life and that of my family.

But God had a different idea. On February 17, 2009 the Lord began to speak to me in the night time hours. During those times it was as though I had been lifted out of my temporal life and taken beyond space and time to the judgment seat of Christ. There Christ sat down with me and conversed with me concerning my life. I asked Him many questions about events and ideas that had affected my life. He was faithful to answer each question in His simple, yet profound way.

During these days of conversation with Jesus, I fell in love with Him and His people in a way that I find hard to communicate. Let me just say that my life will never be the same again. I do not fear death or its author, Satan. Fear and anxiety have been eradicated from my life by visits with Jesus in the heavenly realm. I have seen Jesus and in His presence this temporal realm has faded in importance to me.

I cannot explain how this took place for it is beyond my understanding. I will understand if some do not believe what I have written because I know how incredible it sounds. I only ask that you give it a fair reading and then talk to the Lord about its validity. If you hear from Him you will know the truth.

Paul was caught up to Paradise and could not even speak of it in the first person. He said, "I know a man in Christ who fourteen years ago—whether in the body I do not know, God knows—such a one was caught up to the third heaven" (2 Cor. 12:2). Neither could he tell whether he was in the body or out of the body (v. 3).

Paul was told things that he was not to repeat (2 Cor. 12:4). I do not share everything that Jesus said to me. Some things He does not allow me to share and others are so deeply personal that they are kept between Christ and me.

Upon hearing the voice saying "Come up here" John says, "Immediately I was in the Spirit" (Rev. 4:2) and he began to receive visions of heaven. On February 17 I too was "in the Spirit" and Christ appeared and began to speak to me. I cannot explain it nor will I try.

I share these things so that you may know that my experience may not be totally out of line with how God works. On the other hand, like Paul, I find it hard to explain. What happened is as real to me as my own life. I pray that it will bless all who read.

Because He meets with me in the future, the time element can sometimes be confusing to the reader. Sometimes He speaks in the past tense as if an event has already occurred and other times He speaks as if He is with me in my present time. The reader should be aware of this aspect of the narrative or confusion may result.

Jesus gave me permission to use creative license in presenting these accounts of our conversations. He spoke with me in the night and in the morning I would take out my laptop and write what He told me. Some of the events and words have been subjected to that creative license but I can assure you that the accounts are true as I recalled them.

I am not claiming, as a result of these meetings with Christ, to have some kind of special revelation from God. I ask all who read to follow Paul's warning to "Test all things; hold fast what is good" (1 Thess. 5:21). Do not accept what people tell you without putting it to the test of God's word. What God shares in His word is of much more importance than all of the experiences people can or will have.

Don't simply pass these words through the judgment of your limited doctrinal understanding. Go to God's word for the evidence. Then judge as the Spirit directs.

These visits with the Lord have filled me with a deep desire to proclaim Christ and His eternal purpose to all who will listen. I will proclaim it in any way He commands until I go to meet Him in the heavenly realm once again.

I invite you to come with me into His presence and enjoy the life of fearless joy He offers. Come and enjoy the challenge and blessing of following the Master.

† Chapter 1: How it all Began

It is hard to fathom heaven. It is harder still to imagine sitting down with Jesus Christ at the great judgment seat to discuss one's life as seen through His gracious, loving memory. Most of us in our religious contemplation picture a great throne where Christ is seated In His glorious white robe of judgment. We imagine a long line of people going on for miles waiting their turn to receive the judgment of Christ on the lives they have lived. We imagine some kind of great pronouncement and perhaps a dispensing of rewards.

I believe that it has come to me by way of the Spirit that it will not quite be like that. I am writing this story during a great battle in my life. I am fighting cancer for the third time. At this point I have lost over fifty pounds and am struggling to recover from great weakness.

Through this ordeal of suffering God has opened up the ears of my spirit in such a way that He is taking me beyond temporal restraints into a place and time in the future when He sits down with me to discuss my life. This story is the account of the conversations we have over a period of time.

The Lord awakened me from sleep on the night of February 17, 2009. There in the quiet of the night He began to unfold to me my life as He will have seen it when we meet at His great judgment seat. Each time He spoke I was continually brought to tears as I realized how much I had missed in my life's journey because I had not always had this intimacy with Him. But His compassion and mercy always rose to help me realize that I had been called with a destiny and everything in my life was always turned back to that destiny.

Now, about the judgment seat of Christ. When I talked to the Lord about it He said it was the very same seat that covered the ark of the covenant, often referred to as the mercy seat. When giving His instructions to Moses for the temple He had said, "And there at the mercy seat I will meet with you, and I will speak with you from above the seat" (Ex. 25:22). The seat was stained with the blood of atonement that had been sprinkled by high priests over the years. Golden cherubim spread their wings of protection over the blood-stained covering of the ark.

In the days of the earthly temple the mercy seat was a place of communication between God and His people. His desire has always been to be with His people and talk with them. All of redemption's great plans had been aimed at the restoration of relationship with God. It was a place from which God dispensed mercy and not judgment.

The great seat looked forward to the cross, God's loving act of merciful redemption that set all of creation free from the power of darkness. The heavenly mercy seat was always guarded by real cherubim, mighty guarding angels who attend to the will of God.

When I began to reflect on this from my perspective of Christ's earthly ministry I saw something about Christ that I had not seen clearly during my years on earth. During His ministry Jesus practiced daily exactly what He was doing for me at the mercy seat. Almost always, when He dealt with people He restored them not through religious fanfare but by merely sitting with them and having a conversation. His calm, demeanor and loving ways resulted in people being touched at the deepest level and being healed from within by the Holy Spirit.

When Jesus met the woman of Samaria at the water well He did not preach at her with a condescending voice but merely struck up a conversation. He knew of her brokenness caused by sexual promiscuity and that she was deeply wounded in her heart. As they quietly talked at the well He was able to somehow touch her at the level of her brokenness and set her free.

The next thing we know this formerly devastated woman with an empty life was proclaiming Christ to the people of the city. Now her life had special meaning that she eagerly shared with others. Many in the city believed in Christ through her words and they invited Him to stay with them for two days so they could talk some more. All of this happened because Jesus sat down to talk to a woman at the well (John 4:.7f). A life was changed through a sit-down talk with the Lord.

In a visit with Lazarus, Mary, and Martha, Jesus sat down with the family to quietly and informally speak with them before supper. Mary came to sit at the feet of Jesus and hear from Him. Martha was preparing the meal. Mary realized what many today fail to see. The important thing is to sit at the feet of Jesus and hear from Him. Jesus helped Martha to realize the one thing that was important—conversing with the Christ (Luke 10:42).

When Jesus talked with people He was able to set them free. After His resurrection He was joined on the road to Emmaus by two disciples. They did not recognize Him as they walked along the road talking with Jesus. When they came to their house they invited Him to come and stay with them and have a meal. In the process of their fellowship around a meal their eyes were opened and they recognized Christ. Perhaps many of us do not have a clear revelation of Christ because we will not sit with Him in intimate fellowship.

On another post-resurrection occasion Jesus met His disciples on the shore of the sea. They had fished all night without success and were coming in with no fish in their nets. Jesus cried out to them, "Children, do you have anything to eat?" (John 21:5).

Here was Christ in His resurrection body and His primary interest was to sit down and have breakfast and fellowship with His friends. This is the Jesus I have come to know through the experiences I describe in this story. He wants to meet with us regularly around a meal and converse with us. He wants to touch us at the point of our deepest needs by speaking His healing words. We need to sit down and listen.

I pray for God's people to understand the simple significance of this amazing truth. Jesus simply wants to come into our midst and fellowship with us. Today most of our churches miss this point by building large buildings and hiring preachers to preach eloquent sermons Sunday after Sunday.

We meet in gatherings too large to facilitate the intimate, loving way that Jesus wants to meet with us. Jesus is left at the door of the building and no one seems interested in inviting Him in for a conversation and a meal. He waits at the doors of our religious houses while the people inside continue in their brokenness because they ignore the One who can heal them through the words of a simple conversation. Jesus wants to meet with us but we simply use Him as a means of drawing people into our fruitless programs.

It was not so in the beginning. The first followers of Christ in the early church simply met in small groups in homes. Jesus was the guest of honor in these gatherings and through the Holy Spirit He was able through simple fellowship to transform the lives of those present. Doctor Luke tells us "They continued steadfastly in the apostles' teaching, and fellowship, in the breaking of bread and in prayers" (Acts 2:42).

They gathered around a meal because Christ had so often gathered with them during a meal. There was no program to follow. They simply enjoyed one another's company as they listened to Christ through the teaching of the apostles and by the Spirit. They talked and shared and prayed and sang songs together. In these informal gatherings where Christ was at the center, peoples' lives were transformed by spending time with the Master.

I came to discover through my conversations with Christ at the mercy seat that every gathering of the church is meant to be a gathering at that same seat of mercy. Our gatherings are to be encounters with the Master where He facilitates healing of spirit, soul and body and transforms us into His holy image.

The Lord spoke of a time in the latter days when such gatherings with Him would be the means by which the end time church would be revived and restored for its last glorious ministry to planet earth. His words gave me great hope for the church and His eternal purpose for her.

This story is about my appointed time of fellowship with Christ at the mercy seat. He came to me in the Spirit to have a sit-down talk with someone He loves. So, this entire story unfolds at the great seat of mercy, the judgment seat of Christ, the place where Christ meets with His people to talk with them. It is a conversation between a normal follower of Christ and His God. It is God's account of my life as seen through His eyes of mercy and love.

Some may wonder how such personal conversations could have anything to do with them. You will see as you read that God has a message for the whole body of Christ through these face to face meetings.

Because I have a place as a messenger to His church, the Lord answers my questions in a way that reaches into the hearts of His people. My responses to the Lord echo my deep love for His body and for His truth. These are not private conversations that you are intruding on. He invites you to enter the conversations and hear what He has to say.

† Chapter 2: My Journey to the Judgment Seat

On the night of February 17, 2009 I found myself in the realm of the Spirit. Somehow an experiential memory had been imparted to me. Earth's temporal history had come to a close. Earth and heaven were now united under the rule of the King of the Universe. The great war that brought the ages to their climactic conclusion had been fought and won by the mighty warring Lamb of God who teamed with His army of faithful and the angelic hosts to bring down and defeat the ancient enemy of God. All of heaven seemed primed for a coming event referred to as the celebration of the champions. Anticipation was in the air as we waited for this glorious event.

I had long since visited with my loved ones who had come into the heavenly kingdom, many before me and many who came later. Mary and I and the children and grandchildren and the extended family had experienced a wonderful family reunion filled with love and joy too immense to describe.

With joy unspeakable I had walked the beautiful paths of the heavenly realm with my mother and father who had come into glory many years earlier. We were able to reminisce about our brief life together on earth and the many issues that formed our concerns at the time. Tears flowed as repentance and forgiveness cleansed all that the past had wrought. Eternity was here and its glories were in eternal abundance.

Suddenly, a heavenly surprise changed everything. I was enjoying a quiet walk in a beautiful region with flowing mountain streams and pristine meadows teaming with life. I was immediately blinded by a magnificent light that appeared from above and engulfed me in its blissful glory. The expansive wings of two mighty angelic beings covered me from above like a living canopy. The sound of their wings was like the sound of God's voice carried in the wind caused by their majestic movement. I was stunned and fell to the ground.

These mighty cherubim spread their mighty wings and lifted straight up into the heavens and I was lifted with them and carried to a secret and special place. When my eyes could see again and my body's strength returned, I saw that the glorious angelic beings had stationed themselves above a beautiful golden ark. It was made of brilliant heavenly gold but was stained dark red on the top and sides. The cherubim seemed to be standing guard without the slightest movement.

From a distance I could see someone approaching. Instantly I knew that it was Jesus, my Lord and King. He was clothed with His robe of glory which seemed somewhat muted for my benefit. My knees buckled and my body strength drained away as I realized He was coming to me. I fell to the ground with no strength in my body. He was walking up to me as any man would walk up to another, His hand extended in greeting.

"Stand up son, and let me hold you," He quietly said to my stunned astonishment.

As I started to stand my knees buckled again as I saw the terrible scar in His outstretched hand. Even as I write these words my body is a burning mass of nerves as I recall that moment. The scar seemed to bring all of the reality of earth's great struggle and deposit it into my heart. I could barely breathe. I inherently knew that this scar and the evil associated with it were caused by my sin.

"Let Me help you," Jesus said as His scar-marred hand grasped mine and He lifted me up to Himself. He released my hand and immediately embraced me with a loving hug that saturated me with His calming presence. Of course I returned the loving embrace that dispelled my fears and helped me gain my composure in the presence of the Creator of the universe. It took a long while for it all to sink in.

Jesus gestured toward a beautiful chair that was especially positioned for me next to the golden ark with its red-stained cover. I sat down and noticed that He quietly and purposefully sat down on the mercy seat of the ark.

"I've come to meet with you and speak with you here at the mercy seat, My judgment seat," He said in a stern, strong voice.

"But Lord," I began with deep concern, "with all the great heroes of the faith at your disposal, why would you choose to meet with me?"

"I am meeting with you because you are My son and My brother, and I love you," He calmly replied. "Besides, I meet with all of My precious ones to have this talk at this special place."

"Yes sir," I responded out of my earthly conversation habits.

Jesus just smiled at me as any person would smile at a good friend. And then He continued: "I've come to talk to you about your life. I want you to know how the events of your earthly life lined up with the destiny I assigned to you and how they contributed to My eternal purpose. Don't be fearful, but this talk we will now have is My judgment of your life."

Because of His calming presence, I wasn't fearful but the word "judgment" hit my heart like a bolt of electricity. Here I was seated before My Lord and Master and He was about to speak His judgment over my life. Thoughts swirled around in my soul: What would He say about my sins and the rebellious times of my life? What form would His judgment take? I waited for the answers.

Knowing my thoughts, the Lord, in His matter-of-fact way, replied, "We will talk about anything that comes to your heart as our time together unfolds, including the times of rebellion and sin. But know this, your sins are covered by My atoning blood. I died for your sins and they are not included in this judgment. And yet, we may talk about them so that you will better understand your life and how it unfolded. Our time here at the mercy seat is for you because I love you and I love truth and the freedom it brings."

As He spoke about His blood, my eyes turned to the mercy seat covered with streams of crimson color running from the top to the base of the great ark.

Sensing my thoughts He answered my unspoken plea, "Yes, these are the stains of My blood. After My resurrection I came here as High Priest of heaven to offer My own blood as an everlasting atonement for the sins of the world. Anyone who avails themselves of this blood through faith will never face the judgment of sin. I am sad for those who reject My offer but filled with joy for those who accept it."

Comfortable in His presence now I quietly replied, "I think the Book of Hebrews told us of this great event."

"Yes," He continued as if wanting His point to be made very clear, "The apostle wrote accurately of the event."

When He spoke the words of His own great redemptive document written by His courageous apostles, His voice seemed to rise to a special level of respect. The words flowed from His lips like a heavenly poem spoken for the first time:

> Now, one time at the end of earth's ages, He has appeared to put away sin by the sacrifice of Himself. And as it is appointed for men to die once, but after this comes the judgment, so Christ was offered once to bear the sins of many (Heb. 9:26-28).

As the last words of the apostle flowed from His lips the Lord's eyes seemed to look off into a special faraway place within His own heart. Gradually the serious expression faded and a slow smile formed on His lips. Slowly, His gaze returned to me.

"And now, son," He quietly asked, "what would you like to talk about?"

† Chapter 3: My Destiny

"Lord, earlier you mentioned that this meeting will be about how my life lined up with the destiny you established for my life. Your word says that God chose us in you before the foundation of the world and somehow you established our destiny," I quietly responded. "I don't understand what that means and how it can be."

At my question Jesus let out a small but joyful laugh. My question had been a serious one so I was startled to hear His laughter. And yet His expression of joy brought a sense of comfort.

"Excuse My amusement but I have heard that question so many times from My beloved ones that I cannot help but laugh when I hear it," Jesus responded. "One can only understand destiny by the Holy Spirit. It involves the nature of eternity. The human mind cannot conceive of eternity. But by revelation from My Holy Spirit eternity is as normal as life."

"Lord, I still don't understand," I replied.

"Of course you don't," He continued. "Did I not tell the Samaritan woman at the well, 'The true worshipers will worship the Father in spirit and in truth? For the Father is seeking such to worship

Him. God is spirit, and those who worship Him must worship in spirit and truth'" (John 4:23).

I waited for Him to answer His own question.

"You cannot know God apart from the enlightenment of the Spirit. For ages people tried to know me with their finite minds to no avail. In their attempts to know me through their fleshly minds they created religion. Religion is an attempt to know Me apart from the Spirit."

He paused for a moment and then continued, "Let me explain your destiny from My perspective in the Holy Spirit."

His eyes now seemed to go back to a faraway but very special moment before time as His hushed voice recalled a gathering before the foundation of the world.

"In that time before the beginning, the Father, Son and Holy Spirit gathered to plan the ages of earth. God is love and it is our nature to extend that love to others. Our plan was to create a corporate loving bride for Me. That bride would be the means by which the forces of evil that were to come would be defeated and My glory, through their victorious lives, would fill the earth. The Father's intention from the beginning was that all things in heaven and earth would be brought under My headship as the Christ. I was anointed for that purpose."

The Lord paused and glanced at me knowing that I still struggled to understand.

I took that moment to ask, "Lord, if this is true why did earth's ages result in such sin, and war and chaos?"

"Because we wanted children with a free heart able to choose and love of their own volition," He quickly answered. "Giving humanity the ability to choose meant that we would have to deal with the consequences of them choosing wrongly. We knew this from the beginning because we understand love and the cost it demands. I was anointed as the Christ to be the One who would pay the price to secure a bride who chose to love Me. Such love and unity would accomplish the eternal purpose of God."

Amazingly my spirit was beginning to see what He was saying. "Lord, how did you choose me in that day when the Godhead met?"

With quiet compassion He responded. "You were created in our hearts on that day. You were assigned a place and a time to enter earth's history. At the same time you were given a destiny, an assignment to fulfill during your days on earth. Each person was assigned such a purpose. Your success or failure on earth would be dependent upon whether or not you fulfilled your assigned destiny."

"But Lord how would we come to know and identify that destiny?" I interjected.

"At the appointed time I revealed it to you. When you were a young man of eighteen I touched your heart and revealed my purpose for your life. Do you remember that day?"

"Yes, Lord. I remember seeing something deep in my spirit of your eternal purpose. I saw your bride and the love she had for you. I saw a church rise from the ashes of defeat to walk in loving unity as a sign to the world that you were truly sent from the Father. I did not know how I saw it but I saw it clearly that day."

"Wonderful!" The Lord exclaimed when He heard me speak of that day of revelation. "But with that revelation came the responsibility of your works. Remember how Paul put it: 'For we are His workmanship, created in Christ Jesus unto good works prepared beforehand that we should walk in them' (Eph. 2:10). In that moment in eternity past I prepared your assignment. Receiving the revelation was the beginning of your search to fulfill those works of destiny. The rest of your days would be spent seeking the fulfillment of that destiny and the works it required."

"Lord, it seems to me that if you placed the destiny within me that I had no choice but to fulfill it," I said.

His answer was immediate. "You are forgetting the principle of free choice. Love cannot be birthed or exist where choice is not present. Many chosen ones made the decision to reject their destiny. Like Esau, who sold his birthright for a bowl of stew, they squandered their calling for selfish reasons. Many sold themselves to the enemy and forsook their destiny for the sake of momentary fame and riches. It is a great shame but again this was a price we were willing to pay for true love chosen freely. I was destined to have a bride who loved Me out of the freedom of her heart."

This talk of free choice spurred a question. I hesitated but began, "Lord, I ..."

Sensing my hesitation He interrupted me with the answer I sought to a personal question. "I know, Son. You're concerned about your own faithfulness and what it means for your own judgment. I must tell you that only the Father knows the final answer to that question. In the divine council before time it was reserved to Him for purposes you will one day understand. For now, know that I eagerly wait with you for that outcome. It will be wonderful, regardless."

"I'm content to know that the answer to my judgment lies in the heart of the Father," I quietly responded. "After all He's the One who had to give you to the cross because of My sin."

Jesus smiled with a smile that seemed to brighten heaven. I rested in the peace of that smile.

† Chapter 4: My Childhood Years

The Lord suggested the next topic of our conversation with a tender comment. "I saw that you had a wonderful visit with your parents in the mountains of forgiveness," He said with a look of deep concern.

For a lover of the mountains during my earthly journey the mountains of forgiveness I had seen earlier were an amazing blessing. There were beautiful bubbling streams flowing in and out of the most stunning meadows. Birds flitted everywhere making their joyful noises. The moist smell of dampened soil mingled with the pine aroma of the evergreens and the sweet smell of countless gorgeous heavenly flowers filled my nostrils. The sound of the sparkling stream reminded me of fishing trips I had experienced with my son, Matthew.

I was peering intently up the pathway trying to locate a stately buck deer that I had seen earlier when my eyes fixed on two people seated on a bench beside the pathway. My parents were quietly waiting there looking up the pathway as if expecting to see me. I immediately began to choke with emotion and years of suppressed tears welled up in my eyes.

With big smiles my parents waved eagerly and stood to greet me. I ran to meet them and we did a group hug and cried and cried with tearful joy. I hugged and kissed my mother repeatedly as the years of absence spilled out of my heart.

"I love you mom," I repeated over and over as we caught up on years of deferred love.

"I love you too, son, and I've missed you so," she lovingly responded.

When my eyes turned directly to my father we did not immediately embrace but simply stood and stared at one another with tear-filled eyes and tingling emotion. Then, almost in tandem, we embraced with a father-son embrace that began the healing of over four decades of separation.

I had only known my father when he was in his thirties and I was a young boy. I had always called him daddy. "Daddy, I have missed you so much. To see you here now before my very eyes is…" but my emotion choked away my words.

"It's good to see you, son, after all these years," he began. "I'm sorry I had to leave you so early in your life."

We talked for what seemed like hours mostly looking back at events in our lives that we wished could have been different. I had always regretted not talking to my mother late in her life about personal matters. I had never talked to her about her early life with my father—what it was like when they dated, how difficult it must have been when he left for the war, the kinds of music they listened to and so on. Somehow in the devastation of my father's death these personal matters were hidden and forgotten in the pages of time. She had a stroke late in life and could no longer communicate, so these matters were lost to me.

But on this glorious heavenly day these matters were discovered again and bubbled up freely into our time together in the meadow. Past hurts were buried in the sea of forgiveness and we were refreshed in spirit for an eternity of love together.

My father talked much of his experiences in the war and how they affected him. As a young boy I pleaded with him to tell about the war but the pain of his experiences made it impossible. I had seen the movie *Saving Private Ryan* and wondered what it would have been like to talk to my father after he had grown older. Now in the heavenly forest he talked freely of the events of the war and how they affected him.

As a history teacher I was caught up in his spell-binding accounts of historic events he had seen with his own eyes. His first day on the battlefield was, ironically, on his birthday March 6, 1945. I was five days old on that day having been born on March 1, 1945. He was in the 346th infantry, company L. When he entered the war his regiment had just fought through the infamous Siegfried Line and was preparing for the crossing of the Rhine River.

My father had trained as a caterpillar operator who helped with clearing the supply roads and making roads where needed. This was how he earned a living for us after the war, clearing logging roads and leveling farm land. After the Rhine crossing they had marched across Germany and were surprised to hear of the surrender of Germany on May 7. He shared eagerly of these events since the pain of the war had long since been healed by the hand of God.

I even had a surprise to share with him. Many years earlier my daughter Karis and her husband Jim had helped me discover many facts about my father's military service. In their research they uncovered something amazing. An M1 Garand rifle from the war was on display at the Springfield, Massachusetts armory. To our amazement the rifle turned out to be the same rifle my father had carried in the war. He had carved his name and some other details on the stock making it possible to identify it as his rifle. At the time this seemed like such an amazing coincidence. Of course I now knew God had arranged this to encourage me and help me deal with the loss of my father years earlier.

I was startled out of my thoughts of this meeting by the Lord's gentle question, "Do you wonder why your father was taken from you at an early age?"

"Yes Lord, I have never understood that," I calmly responded.

His answer was a quote from His word: "For everything there is a season, and a time for every purpose under heaven: a time to be born and a time to die" (Eccl. 3:1, 2).

"I know that passage Lord," I replied, "but I still wonder why some people seem to have been robbed of their full opportunity on earth."

His response was very clear: "I chose these times and seasons but not always by choice. Man's choice of rebellion created a chaos that I was forced to use for My purpose. Many innocent aborted babies were destroyed even before they had an opportunity to be born. Wars took many children and other innocent bystanders. In My infinite wisdom I took the chaos caused by sin and worked it for ultimate good."

"But Lord, my father…" I started to object when Jesus interrupted me with a paraphrase from the same passage.

"I make all things beautiful in their time and I have put eternity into the heart of man. The aborted children are here with us in glory. Satan tried to kill off a generation of children but I caused his hate to fill heaven with the sound of joyful children playing. I used your father's untimely death to produce in you a wealth of grace that you just now understand. I put eternity in your hearts so that you would be able to see past earth's chaos into the clarity of eternity."

And so I began to see my childhood years in a different light. I saw that God had used those years to slowly build into my life the building blocks that would eventually lead me to the fullness of my appointed destiny.

God truly does make all things beautiful in their time.

† Chapter 5: Joining the Family of God

"Lord, I remember when I first met you," I said, as I changed the subject.

"Of course I remember that day as well," the Lord responded. "All of heaven rejoiced when you became my child and entered the heavenly family."

"I had been religious before I met you but I was confused about who you were and what you expected of me," I continued. "I wanted to please you but I wasn't sure how to do it."

"Yes, religion has that affect on people," He assured me. "It distracted many from simply getting to know Me as I am and walking in fellowship with Me. I simply want companionship with My children. Religion portrayed Me in a false way."

I continued on this subject close to my heart. "I remember being so hungry to find the real you in your word. Mary challenged me to see what the Bible really said about you and the salvation you offered. I devoured your word for many weeks as I sorted through what I believed."

With a big smile and a comforting laugh the Lord began to recall the time of my birth into His kingdom. "I remember. You were reading from Paul's letter to the Ephesian believers. Your heart suddenly grasped the true meaning of verses eight and nine of the second chapter."

Then the words of Paul's epistle rolled from His lips like an author reading favorite words from his favorite book: "For by grace you were saved through faith and that not of yourselves for it is a gift of God. Not of works lest any man should boast."

"Those words set me free, Lord. I had always thought that I could only please you by doing certain works. Through these words I saw that you saved me with the same grace I see in you now. You simply came to me and offered yourself to me freely. I was overwhelmed by the freedom that entered my life!"

Basking in His big smile, I paused for a moment and then continued: "Lord, the faith to know you and believe in you seemed to appear out of nowhere. I've always wondered about that."

"Faith," came His revealing answer, "is My gift to those who listen for My voice and hear what I have to say. It is a door in your heart that opens to receive My grace and the benefits of it. The door opened in your heart because you sought My voice in My word. You listened to Me and were able to hear. Then the door of your heart opened and I came in to fill you with My grace and eternal life."

"I remember," I excitedly responded, "bowing down at my bedside and having that first conversation with you. I received your grace through the gift of faith and I was wonderfully set free. I no longer had to worry about pleasing you but realized that you were already pleased with me and accepted me freely."

A big warm smile came to the Lord's face as He lovingly said, "You were a newborn baby in My kingdom. I was pleased with you like any parent is pleased at the sight of their new baby. What you couldn't see at the moment were the angels who had been assigned to you rejoicing in that bedroom. They had witnessed your birth and were dancing and praising God at your entrance into the kingdom. They were dancing through the roof and the walls in their excitement."

"Wow! I was blessed to be born again, but I guess heaven was even more blessed."

"Yes indeed," the Lord agreed, "that was a glorious day for heaven and earth."

We were both silent for a while as I soaked up the goodness of the moment and the Lord just kept smiling and occasionally letting out a little snicker of joy.

Finally, in a concerned tone, I broke the silence: "Lord, I was blessed for many weeks following my spiritual birth but it seemed like I began to flounder sooner than I expected."

The Lord was very quick with His response. "You floundered because you were born into an environment with no incubator."

"No incubator?" I questioned.

"The body of Christ is My incubator for new born spiritual babies," He went on. "But when you were born again the body of Christ was not functioning very effectively. They didn't know how to nourish, and care for new spiritual infants. They knew many things about doctrines, and religious practices but they fell short of being a nourishing company of believers."

"Thankfully it wasn't that way later," I interjected.

"No, Lloyd. In the days prior to the latter days my church began to truly function as the body of Christ. Because of the devastation of the times, they began to rally in smaller groups and genuinely care for one another. They abandoned their religious programs and simply began to meet together in true fellowship with Me as the guest of honor. Those days marked the beginning of the great rising up of My church, My body on earth."

Excitedly I responded, "I hope to be blessed to see the beginning of that rising up of your church. It would be the fulfillment of all I have dreamed of for so many years."

"Son, not only do you get to see it, but you have a significant part to play in that success. You and many others had been planting seeds for this revival for many years. Finally, those seeds began to sprout."

"I'm so glad to know that others later on had the privilege of being born into a healthy family of God," I concluded. "I'm humbled to have been a seed planter and that the seeds brought forth new life."

Jesus smiled and my heart was at peace.

† Chapter 6: Becoming a Follower of Christ

When I was born again into the family of God I made the mistake of thinking that my life would now be totally transformed and I would go on to live victoriously in Christ. I read verses like 2 Corinthians 5:17: "So that if anyone is in Christ, he is a new creation; the old things have passed away. Behold, all things have become new!" One could conclude from this passage that after the new birth experience everything is new, the old has passed away and so everything should be wonderful.

I had struggled in my life to discover what it really means to be a true follower of Christ. What did the Lord really expect of us as His children? As I sat before the Lord this question swirled around in my thinking.

Finally, I asked, "Lord, what must a person do to truly be your follower?"

The Lord's gentle smile gave away that He was pleased to answer my question. "My disciples are those who seek to hear My voice and do My will. They are those who reach a point in their lives that the only thing that matters is pleasing Me in all things."

I responded, "It seems such a simple thing, Lord. I wonder why in reality it is much more difficult."

"The problem lies with the fallen human soul of man. Though you may be born again into My family, your soul is still in its fallen state, totally independent, self-centered, and rebellious. The question of being My disciple involves the required death of your independent soul nature. Without that, one cannot truly follow Me in fullness."

Now the Lord stopped to let His words sink into my thinking. I could see that He was about to open up this subject in a way that would certainly change my life. I was very eager to hear what He had to say.

He slowly continued. "When we created the first humans we created them in our image. The first man and woman were like God in that they were spirit beings in fellowship with God. We walked and talked together in the garden. We had companionship. Through the spirit there was direct communication between us. Nothing separated us from one another. We gave man a body made of the elements of earth so he could enjoy the beauty of creation we had given him."

Now a firm, serious expression crossed the face of my Lord. It was apparent that He was about to disclose something very important and serious. I waited with anticipation.

His words came deliberately. "When we breathed the spirit of life into the physical body of man, he became a living soul. As a soul being man received the right to choose. He was not a mindless being without options but one with the potential of being independent. God is love. His love demanded that His children be free creatures with the ability to think, reason, choose and express emotion. Man's soul was to become the pivotal element of all of creation."

As the Lord paused to lift His heart back to that crucial moment in history I was filled with deep awe knowing that God had taken such an awesome step of love. And yet I knew that this creation of the human soul presented a profound spiritual mystery.

The Lord picked up His explanation of this great mystery. "Adam and Eve had the choices of life in God or life within themselves. Every person has these choices. The tree of life in the garden represented My life. The other tree, the tree of the knowledge of good and evil represented their independent life apart from Me. If they chose, they could cut themselves away from direct companionship with Me and go their own way. The mystery of the independent soul of man—full of potential—full of incredible risk. A risk taken out of divine love—love seeking a free bride who would love Me from the heart."

Can sadness and joy be expressed on the face at the same time? As I fixed my eyes on His face at this point, I knew the answer.

Sadly the Lord picked up the story. "They chose to go their own way. When they disobeyed our command they chose to act out of their independence and separate themselves from direct dependence on God. In essence, they became their own god, able to make their own decisions about good and evil. At that moment of rebellion they died spiritually. Their bodies were alive and their souls were alive but their spirits became fireless lamps, separated from the life of God."

"But Lord," I put in. "Didn't your redemptive plan of the cross restore this fellowship between you and man?"

"The cross answered the dilemma of sin. Through My redemptive death I restored the tree of life. Those who lived before the cross looked forward to it by faith and those who came after it were able to receive Me and My life once again. As I told Nicodemus, 'For God so loved the world that He gave His only begotten Son, that everyone believing in Him should not perish but have everlasting life' (John 3:16). Those who chose to believe in Me were restored to life in Me."

The Lord paused for a brief moment and then quietly continued, "The sin question was answered but the mystery of the independent soul of man remained. To be true followers My people must deal with this issue of the human soul."

Each time the Lord spoke of the human soul my mind went to the time when Peter had confessed Jesus as the Christ and then had almost immediately rejected what Christ said about the way to redemption. Christ had rebuked Peter sternly with the words, "Get behind Me, Satan! You are a hindrance to Me, for you are not setting your mind on the things of God, but the things of men" (Matt. 16:23).

I started to ask the Lord about this but knowing my thoughts He opened up His heart on this crucial issue of following Him. "The things of God and the things of men—this was Peter's issue. Are we moved by the viewpoint of man, flawed by its fallen human nature, or by that of God?"

"But Lord, if our human nature is so corrupt how can a believer ever reach the point of truly following you," I yearned to know. "It seems that our human soul would always win out over the things of God."

"My words to My disciples at the time were a call to true discipleship and the cost it demands. I said to them, 'If anyone would come after Me, let him deny himself, take up his cross and come follow Me. For whoever would save his soul will lose it, but whoever loses his soul for My sake will find it'" (Matt. 16:24-26).

Of course I had read these words many times and had always been awed by their profound importance. As Jesus spoke the words from His own written word, my heart seemed to melt a little at their power.

Then He continued. "There is no answer to the human soul other than death. It must die and experience resurrection. Following Me must begin with the denial of self. How can one follow God when his soul is actively giving counter directions? How can one hear from God when his soul keeps crying out its selfish desires? The soul must, from the beginning, be denied its claim as the false god of the human heart. The independent way introduced by Adam and Eve must be reversed."

The words of Jesus bring life. As His words flowed forth I felt His life strengthening me, even here in the heavenly realm. But the strong commitment His words demanded brought a deep resolve to savor every word. I knew I was receiving revelation that would drastically change my earthly life and that of those around me.

He continued. "To take up your cross is to commit to this death process. I died for your sins and set you free from its power but only you can die to your selfish nature and be free to follow Me. But know this, when you truly lose your selfish soul for My sake, I give to you a resurrected soul, transformed by My life.

"Resurrection follows death. In Me you will find a life of fulfillment beyond your dreams. In Me the heavenly life of victory can be yours. My people do not have to wait for heaven to live the heavenly life. You have been raised up with Me in resurrection life and seated with Me in the heavenly places."

Slowly I let my understanding flow from my mouth. "Lord, the cost of discipleship is great, but the reward is even greater."

"You've said a mouthful, My son. Following Me is both the greatest challenge of the human race and the greatest reward!"

† Chapter 7: A Time of Rebellion

    Our talk at the judgment seat had become so comfortable that sometimes there were times of silence in which we both simply waited on one another for the next subject of our conversation. During one of those times of contemplation I took on a very somber mood and drifted deep into my thoughts. I was pondering a time in my earthly life when I had rebelled against God. I had rejected His presence and drifted off into a very lustful time.
    My mind was constantly bombarded with perverted thoughts of sex in those days and no matter what I did I couldn't break free. God became distant to me because I was ashamed of my behavior and I could not face Him. There were times when I would go through the motions of repentance but deliverance never came. There was a battle going on in my mind and I was losing it daily.
    Jesus knew my thoughts and seemed very sad for the pain He knew I was experiencing. But He waited for me to speak first.
    It is strange that I could feel shame for my sin at the very place Jesus offered His blood for my sins. The shame was tying my tongue in knots and closing off my heart. But then I looked into the eyes of my Lord and I could see at once two things: the deep hurt that sin had caused Him and overwhelming compassion for my well being.

And so I opened my mouth and began to tell Him what He already knew. Though I had confessed these things to Him long ago in my earthly life and had gained the victory over them, I sensed that He wanted to bring an eternal sense of finality to that time in my life.

As tears welled up my heart spilled out to my Redeemer: "Lord, more than anything about that terrible time I regret turning my back on you and cutting myself off from your presence."

"Those were sad times for our relationship. I was grieved, the Holy Spirit was grieved and your angels were grieved to see you walk away from Me," He sternly responded.

"Lord, help me understand what happened," I pleaded.

After a contemplative pause the Lord began: "In the middle of earth's twentieth century My adversary devised a massive plan of attack against America. His plan unleashed an army of demons whose mission was to introduce wealth and pleasure as the answers to happiness. Many of these demons were assigned to introduce sexual perversion and a twisted view of family and marriage."

"Obviously his plan worked," I quietly broke in.

"Yes indeed, and you and many others became victims of this massive strategy. Of course you realize that this does not excuse your behavior but only explains the demonic source of it."

"But Lord, how did I open up to this strategy of the enemy?" I wanted to know.

"Demons entered peoples' lives through wounds in the soul. Where there was unhealed hurt they had entrance into your life," He explained.

"I remember being seriously hurt as a result of our trip to the east coast," I responded. "We had traveled there with great hope for the church we were part of. Instead our time there proved to be a grave disappointment. We returned with deep wounds and anger against what we perceived to be the church."

"This disappointment," replied Jesus, "clashed with the revelation of the church that I had put within your heart. Suddenly you doubted that the revelation was real."

"Yes," I agreed. "I remember symbolically throwing the revelation you had given me to the ground and kicking dirt on it. I didn't want to have anything more to do with it."

Sadly, the Lord replied, "And while your call to destiny lie covered with dirt you turned your back on Me and struck out on your own."

When I saw the sadness in the eyes of my Lord I began to weep with sorrow. Here I was concerned about my days of rebellion and He was the One who was hurt the most. We forget that, though our Lord is the all powerful God, He has deep feelings for us. He can be deeply grieved by how we treat Him. He loves us so much and has invested Himself into our lives so that we can prosper and be blessed in Him.

The Lord touched me gently on the shoulder and touched my heart with His next words: "But I would not let your calling lie in the dust. I picked it up, brushed it clean, and returned it to your reluctant hands. You had the choice of throwing away your destiny or merely ignoring it but I wanted it to be in your life daily reminding you that you had a real connection with eternity."

"Lord, I now know this rebellion carried over into my ministry as pastor," I confessed. "Instead of working to instill your vision of your church into the people I developed selfish motives and took credit for the things you were doing in our midst."

"So many of My shepherds thought they could proceed using their own ingenuity and creativity. They were moved by their own vision instead of My voice," the Lord explained with some sadness in His voice.

"I know that I stopped listening to you during those days. I thought I had the prerogative of just doing what I thought would work," I said.

"You forgot that it is My church and not yours—that I could only build it if you listened to my voice and let me lead the way. During My earthly ministry I did nothing of Myself. I only did what I saw the Father doing. I was submitted to His will. Likewise your task was to do only what you saw Me doing. You were to have ears to hear what I was saying and then have the courage to obey."

"Lord, I am ashamed that I did not learn that lesson earlier," I said with my eyes downward.

"You fell prey to the spirits of the age that worshipped self and promoted wealth and pleasure. Many of my shepherds fell from the high places to which they allowed themselves to ascend. Your pride allowed you to take my glory and pride comes before a great fall."

Now humbled by the Lord's words I quietly responded, "I fell flat on my face. When you revealed to me my selfish motives I was embarrassed by my presumptuous attitude."

"And that" the Lord said with finality, "was the beginning of a journey into a wilderness into which I would lead you. In the wilderness I would restore you but it would not be easy. Like unrefined gold I would place you in the crucible to be refined for My purpose."

At that point our conversation shifted to an ominous subject.

† Chapter 8: Into the Wilderness

As we both pondered this next exchange in quiet contemplation, I was rolling that word "crucible" around in my mind. I knew that a crucible was a cauldron in which gold ore was placed and heated to high temperatures so that the impure dross could be separated from the pure gold. The gold was really useless until it was extracted from the impure particles of the ore.

As I saw it, this process demanded two things: major heat through fire, and a separation process. The dross was lighter than gold and would rise to the surface when boiled, where it was skimmed away from the pure gold. The gold, then, could be poured into forms and cooled to await the time when it would be fashioned into fine jewelry.

As usual Jesus knew my thoughts. As I was contemplating His word "crucible" He had been watching me intently. He knew that I was remembering a very trying time in my Christian walk.

"I see you're remembering the time when I took you into the wilderness to face the refining fire," He quietly interjected.

"Yes, Lord, I remember how confused I was when you began that process," I answered. "Mary and I both were lost and confused as you separated us from the structured church and isolated us for your purpose."

"The wilderness is the crucible I spoke of," He went on. "I take My servants into the wilderness to break them of their dependency on self and refine them for My purpose."

"I finally came to see the wisdom of your statement, Lord. At first it was difficult to understand and accept but as time went on I saw what the wilderness was doing in my heart. Many of my fellow Christians did not understand it at all and thought I had gone off the deep end in my spiritual walk."

The Lord looked sternly into my eyes and continued: "I led many of my servants into the wilderness to ready them for their calling in Me. I chose Moses to lead My people to freedom but at the age of forty he was not ready for the challenge. His selfish flesh had developed out of control in his power position as a leader in Egypt. He showed this by killing the Egyptian who was oppressing one of his brethren. He meant well but he took matters into his own hands because that was all he knew. He did not know how to hear My voice and be led by it."

"So then you led Moses into the wilderness," I said the obvious.

"Yes," He continued, "I needed to get Moses out of the environment of Egypt where his flesh prospered. Then I would allow the harsh desert to work its refining work on his soul. He entered the desert a confident, strong man in his natural strength. When he was ready to return to Egypt to fulfill his destiny, he was a humble man who had lost confidence in his flesh.

"When I appeared to him through the burning bush I had to convince him that he was capable of the mission I was giving him. The wilderness had broken him down and now I would build him back up and send him forth in My power. Now he was ready to be used by his God. The wilderness had worked its wonders."

"Then when he did lead Israel to freedom he did so in your power and authority," I added. "His only weapons were a staff and faith in you."

"You are exactly right, Lloyd," He said, affirming me. "I could use him because his soul had been refined in the crucible of the hot dry wilderness."

"Lord, I was thinking about how you prepared David in a wilderness as well," I said, desiring to hear it from His own lips.

"Yes, David was anointed as king at a very young age but he was not ready to be king. Like Moses he had much natural strength of body and soul that would not serve him well as king over My people. I sent him into the wilderness of Adullam where he gathered with the outcasts of the land in caves. In the caves he gained humility and learned to trust in my strength and to be led by My Spirit. When he stepped into his destiny as king he had the heart of a shepherd rather than a warrior. He became a great warrior because his heart was in tune with mine."

"Your word speaks of many others prepared by the wilderness," I added.

"Joseph I readied for the fulfillment of his dream in the dungeons of Egypt. In the dark gloominess of the prison his proud soul was shaped and refined for a great mission. He rose to become a mighty leader in Egypt not because of his natural ability but because he finally submitted his will to mine. Joseph's brothers committed a great sin in selling their brother into slavery. But I used this great evil to prepare him for his destiny."

The Lord paused now and looked off into the past as he no doubt pondered many who had served Him faithfully during their earthly journeys. That big smile filled His face as He remembered their faithfulness.

Quietly, He continued, "I sent Paul into the regions of Arabia, Syria and Cilicia, to prepare him apart from the influence of others. I put the revelation of My purpose within him and used the wilderness to ready his heart for my message. Paul was highly trained and knowledgeable but eventually he came to see that his natural ability would not serve him well. His own words reveal how he came to embrace this truth:

> But what things were gain to me, these I have counted loss for Christ. Indeed I count everything as loss because of the surpassing worth of knowing Christ Jesus my Lord. For His sake I have suffered the loss of all things and count them as rubbish in order that I may gain Christ' (Phil. 3:7, 8).

I reflected on the Lord's seriousness about this subject as I reacted to what He had just said: "It seems that your servants could not really begin to serve you until they were able to deny self and fully embrace your purpose."

The Lord was shaking His head slowly in agreement with me and then in a serious tone he added this: "Even I had to deny myself in readiness for My ministry. Following My baptism and empowerment by the Holy Spirit, I was led by the Spirit into the wilderness (Matt. 4:1). I denied myself food and water and resisted the enemy's temptations to use self as a source.

"From that moment on I only did what I saw the Father doing. I constantly was moved not by My will but by the will of Him who sent Me. I submitted fully to the Father. The wilderness prepared Me to do My Father's business while denying My own will."

I was humbled and quieted by the Lord's words. Long ago I had come to accept the Lord's wisdom in leading me into a wilderness, but now in this special place ringing with His wise words I understood fully what He had done for me. The wilderness had brought much pain but now I saw how fully it had worked His purpose into my life.

But the Lord wanted me to hear it from His own lips one final time: "Son, like all of my other servants, I had to separate you from your source of natural strength. Your position as pastor fed your strong ego. You were an eloquent speaker and you had gained much knowledge. Like Paul you had much to take credit for. I revealed to you your selfish motives in the midst of that ministry and you were shocked to see how you had robbed Me of My glory."

He paused for a moment realizing that I was cringing a bit at His words. He reached out His scarred hand to touch me on the shoulder. His touch assured me that all of this past indiscretion was covered by His redeeming blood. He didn't say a word. He merely glanced down at the mercy seat with its stains of blood. I understood.

Then He quietly continued: "I led you to a town called Atascadero which means mud hole. It was truly a spiritual mud hole for you and Mary. The believers there did not honor your natural abilities. Close friends abandoned you. The churches did not embrace you. Your eloquence was put on a shelf and your Bible knowledge became useless for a while. Finally you were rejected by the organized church. You began to discover that your message would not be accepted by those who continued to live by expediency and natural strength. Your message became a threat to the religious kingdom they had built."

"I remember it as a time of spiritual dryness where your voice seemed distant. I yearned for your presence but it seemed that you had stepped back from our lives to allow the crucible to refine our hearts," I replied solemnly.

The Lord's compassion was obvious as He moved on to a big turning point in our lives. "And then I allowed cancer to enter your lives," He said quietly in a very matter of fact tone.

"Those were difficult times for us when I developed cancer the first time. At the time it was extremely hard to understand how it fit into your plans. I had such strong beliefs about your healing power so it went against much that we believed and held dear."

The Lord was gentle with His words. "Of course you came to understand fully that I did not directly put the cancer upon your body."

"Yes Jesus," I agreed. "I know that disease is the work of your enemy. You despise it because of the hurt and destruction it brings to people. During your ministry you went about healing all who were oppressed by the devil. I know of no situation in your ministry where you refused to heal someone. You healed the sick, and lame, opened blind eyes, raised the dead and cast out the enemy wherever you found him."

Jesus was again smiling His approval of my understanding of His attitude about disease. He knew that I had long since settled the matter in my heart. But I could tell there was something important He wanted to tell me.

And so He began very quietly and deliberately: "Satan could not have put cancer upon your body without My permission. I granted him permission just as I granted him permission to enter the life of Job so many years earlier. I knew two important things that you did not yet see: first, that the cancer would be the final nail in the coffin of your self. During that season you truly began to die to self and let Me reign in your life.

Secondly, you did not know that I was preparing you for a future ministry of healing in which cancer would be your primary target. Later you were able to set many free because of your experience with and knowledge of the spirit of cancer. You learned of its devious ways from personal experience. You were able to turn the table on Satan and defeat him in this important front of the spiritual war."

Of course I had long ago come to understand what the Lord was telling me. But here at the ark of the temple of heaven the words of Jesus brought an eternal finality to this question. As Paul had said, "We know that all things work together for good to those who love the Lord and who are called according to His purpose" (2 Cor. 8:28). I had always loved the Spirit's use of the word "all." It seemed that He wanted us to understand that everything was subject to His will in the lives of His chosen, destined people.

Knowing my thoughts the Lord said softly with finality: "But I did not allow the cancer to destroy you. When it had worked its purpose in you it was removed from your life. You were ready now to stand on your feet and continue your journey in My will."

My brother in Christ, Timm was once given a clear vision that illustrates the principle of the wilderness. The vision shows a target at the top of the page but a zigzag line going up, down and back up toward the target. When we are first saved most of us think that we, as spiritual arrows, will be launched immediately and go in a straight line directly toward the target.

Little did we know that God would allow a downward descent in our spiritual progress during which He would prepare us to hit the target. We want to hit the target immediately but God wants to smooth, straighten, and strengthen us so we would be arrows fashioned in His hands ready to accurately hit His target. Then He puts us into a quiver until He is ready to use us for His purpose. Only then do we get launched toward the target.

The wilderness is real. It is a place of preparation during which God is fashioning us for His purpose we must learn to wait upon Him and let Him prepare us to hit His target.

† Chapter 9: God Clarifies His Purpose

    I have carried the vision of God's eternal purpose for His church in my heart for over forty years. But I was not always clear about how it would manifest itself in the lives of real believers. Knowing the dismal condition of the organized church, I wondered whether God would be able to fulfill His purpose within its confining structure.
    The organized church seemed to me to be the old wineskin that Jesus spoke of in His parable. It seemed to me that the new wineskin was some other form of church life that the Spirit would form for the last days.
    God chose to bring us back to Tollhouse and the church I had once pastored in order to bring His divine clarity to this question. It was as if my spiritual eyes were a telescope and He had adjusted the lens so that I could see with crystal clear vision. I now see clearly, thanks to His clear revelation, the form the church will take in the latter days of planet earth.
    This was a subject I really wanted to talk to Jesus about. I could tell that He perceived this and so I quickly brought up the issue. "Lord, I was remembering the time that you brought us back to the church at Tollhouse."

"Indeed, that was a crucial time in your life," the Lord responded. "I brought you back so that I could return you to the circumstances you had left before your restoration. By that time your heart had been fully restored from the selfish motives that I had revealed to you when you were the pastor."

"I remember returning," I broke in, "with such a naïve attitude about my own restoration of heart. I felt that everyone would be able to see that you had refined me as gold in your wilderness crucible. I just knew that my brothers and sisters there would fully embrace what you had done in my heart and life."

"Instead you received a big surprise," the Lord responded. "It was for that surprise that I returned you to your old church."

"They were not able," I went on, "to receive the message you had put within me, Lord. Through the gift of prophecy that you had given me, I began to speak forth your will for the church. Many in the church recognized that it was you speaking to them. I was sharing the new wine of restoration with the church in hope that the church itself could be restored."

"Until you arrived, you did not know that they had embarked on a program to build a new church building," the Lord reminded me. "As you sought Me in prayer about this I told you then that they had not sought My will about this project. You began to realize that they were headed in a direction away from restoration and revival."

"And then the big surprise came that you had planned for us," I said sadly. "The leadership asked Mary and me to leave the church. Our presence and our message had been rejected outright. They had not recognized any change in my heart and were not willing to consider that they may have missed your best for them."

"And then you understood more fully the challenge that I faced with the religious leaders during my earthly ministry," the Lord said. "The people responded to My message because they were hungry, but the Pharisees and scribes had become satisfied with their stale renditions of religious tradition. I knew by the Spirit that they would not and could not receive My message and My mission as the Christ."

Humbly, I replied: "Lord, I wish I had come to the church with your insight. I was naïve to think that new wine could be poured into an old wineskin. Instead, they simply rejected the new wine and went about their business."

"And that was the clarity I wanted to bring to your heart. You had to see once and for all that organized religion cannot receive the newness of the Spirit. Throughout earth's history this had been proven over and over. When My Spirit would revive the hearts of the people, the organized church would reject what He was doing for the sake of their old traditions.

"Always, the wineskin would burst and the wine was wasted until I could fashion a new container for the new wine. Where hearts are brittle and inflexible revival is impossible. True restoration demands that the fallow ground of the heart be softened by repentance and openness to change."

Jesus had spoken with such clarity on the subject of the wineskin that I wondered why it had taken me so long to get it. I felt I had wasted so much time in the organized church trying to help people see God's glorious plan.

"Your time wasn't wasted," the Lord said as He acknowledged my thoughts. "Always remember that the church is my people. It is not the program that men have built and empowered with self, but individual believers in Me. Controlling men have built fences around My people in order to keep them under their command. They have used my sheep for their own personal agendas apart from consultation with Me. When you entered the fences you brought hope to My people."

I silently pondered what Jesus had just said. Then words seemed to spontaneously glide from my lips: "I was amazed later on in my life how this truth unfolded before my eyes. During the time of the rising up of the church I would witness a mass exodus from the organized church but a real grass roots revival of true church life."

"Yes!" the Lord said excitedly. "Those were exciting days for My bride. I watched her being fitted in her glorious gown and witnessed the spots and blemishes begin to be cleansed. She was escaping from her confinement by religion and beginning to dance in the freedom of My love."

"Lord, I was so blessed to be there to see the beginning of that great miracle," I replied with a smile on my face.

His response was encouraging. "Your smile betrays your heart. I too smile when I consider the amazing miracle the world witnessed after those days—the forming of a new wineskin for the latter days."

† Chapter 10: Hints of Victory

In the early morning of my birthday, March 1, 2009, the Lord spoke to me about a time period He refers to as the rising up of the church. This conversation with the Lord was like a birthday gift to me since the subject is so dear to my heart. Since our conversations take place in the eternal future at the judgment seat of Christ, amazingly I already know by the Spirit and later experience in my life about this remarkable period that is coming to planet earth.

Though the Lord never gives me any definite time references, it is clear to me that this time of the rising of the church begins in my lifetime. It is a time when the Holy Spirit begins to form a new spiritual wineskin—a new expression of His church.

I no longer doubt that the last days of planet earth will witness the emergence of a church that will fulfill the promises and prayers of Jesus. The end of the ages will not be accompanied by a rapture rescue of the people of God from tribulation. In fact it will be the tribulation of those days that will cause the church to rise up in love, unity, and power. I know this goes counter to the thinking of many leaders in the church, but that does not concern me. The word of God is clear on this subject.

Jesus and I sat quietly together. He seemed never to be in a hurry. With my carried-over-from-earth concept of time, it was hard for me to grasp how He could be so relaxed and patient with me when He had so many others to meet with. Time, of course, is not a concept of the eternal realm. God is the Great I Am. He exists now and forever. The word says, "Jesus Christ is the same yesterday, today, and into the ages" (Heb. 13:8). The past, present, and future, as we know them, belong to Him now. There are no constraints of time with Him. He always has time for us—all the time we need.

"Happy birthday," the Lord said ending the quiet moment.

I was immediately struck by the irony of His greeting. Here was the Great I Am who lives in a realm of eternal now and knows no boundaries of time, and yet He remembered and appreciated the day I began my journey on earth. God is so immense and yet He is able to meet us at our points of smallness. It boggles my mind.

"Thank you Lord," I responded. "And thank you for the gift of your revelation of the rising up of the church."

"You're welcome," He responded with His big smile. "I know how much it means to you to know that you would live to see the beginning of this victorious time in the life of My church."

"Lord, in the late twentieth century it seemed that Christians were oblivious to the possibility that your church would experience a great end time restoration. Most people seemed content to simply drift along in spiritual mediocrity while believing that the church would remain in its defeated condition to the end and then be raptured away. I often became frustrated that people could not see what you had said and prayed in your word."

The Lord joined my thinking, "Thankfully in the next century that would begin to change. My word says, 'For where there is no spiritual vision, the people are unrestrained' (Prov. 29:18). Without the revelation of My Spirit that comes to those who seek it, people cannot see the most obvious truths. The church had become self-satisfied and complacent and could not see the apparent. That is why they were so scattered and purposeless in that period of time."

"You spoke many times in your word of this rising up of the church," I said.

"Indeed I did. The moment sin entered the world the Father spoke forth the end of this matter. He said to the deceiver, 'And I will put enmity between you and the woman, and between your seed and her Seed. He shall bruise your head and you shall bruise His heel'

(Gen. 3:15). I am the Seed of this prophecy but many miss the point that the body of Christ is also of this Seed because it is composed of My brothers and sisters.

"I have declared, 'He put all things under His feet and gave Him to be head over all to the church the fullness of Him who fills all in all' (Eph. 1:22, 23). The enemy was destined to be bruised in His head by Me through My spiritual offspring, the church of the living God."

Excited about what the Lord was saying I said, "And that's why Paul wrote that 'the God of peace will soon crush Satan under your feet'" (Rom. 16:20).

"Yes, I was privileged to crush Satan's head but I did it through the feet of My church, the expression of My fullness on earth. In the day of the last battle I worked in perfect concert with My bride, the church, to utterly defeat the enemy. What a victory it was!"

We were both excited now as we relived the great victory of the latter days. It was inspiring to see the Lord's eyes gleam with triumph when He spoke of His great victory through teamwork with His glorious prepared bride.

"Lord," I added, "During my earth walk this question of the church's ultimate victorious rising seemed settled to me by your intercessory prayer before your death. In your prayer you said, 'I do not pray for these alone but also for those who would believe in Me through their word that they all may be one, as You, Father, are in Me and I in You, that they also may be one in Us, that the world may believe that you sent Me.'" (John 17:20, 21).

"That was My ending declaration in prayer for the ultimate victory of My church. The process was simple: The Father was in Me, I was in the Father, and by the Spirit We together were in the church. Finally, the church would become spiritually and actually one and that supernatural oneness would be a testimony to the world that the Father sent Me into the world. That spiritual oneness would result in Satan's defeat as My church rose up in unified faith in My name and power. Satan was no match for a church submitted to My will and expressing My authority in the earth."

His words resounding in my spirit, I simply laid my head back to ponder what the Lord had just said. I had heard these words many times and knew of this end time rising up of the church, but to hear it from the mouth of Jesus was a special joy.

† Chapter 11: The Collapse of America

In the course of these conversations with Jesus it becomes apparent that the great country in which we are blessed to live will suffer a great spiritual, social, financial and cultural collapse. The Lord speaks of this disaster as though it is a precursor to the time He refers to as the rising up of the church. I believe, and some of Lord's comments imply, that my generation will experience the tragic beginning of this collapse.

There was divine seriousness in the Lord's demeanor when we broached this subject. It was apparent as we entered into this discussion that it was a sensitive matter to Him. America had been the first country founded and built upon the moral truths revealed in the word of God. Its collapse was obviously one of the great tragedies of human history.

"I am sad for America," the Lord began. "During a seventy year period this country slowly but deliberately dismantled its moral and spiritual foundation. A structure without a strong and viable foundation will collapse from within."

"Lord, I believe I lived through much of the time you speak of," I responded. "I remember being concerned about the homosexual agenda that seemed to be blasting away at one of the foundation stones of our nation—marriage."

The Lord's response to this issue was immediate and direct: "The greatest error of this movement was that they blatantly accused Me of contributing to the development of sin. I did not put within the human race any genetic proclivity toward sin. "Lucifer, in His rebellion introduced sin and the destruction it brings. Then sin developed in the disobedient hearts of mankind. Those whom I created in My image embraced sin and cultivated it of their own volition. Paul, through My inspiration, wrote of this downfall of the human race:

> For God's wrath is revealed from heaven against all ungodliness and unrighteousness of men, who suppress the truth in unrighteousness, because what may be known of God is clearly known within them, for God revealed it to them. For since the creation of the world His invisible attributes are clearly seen, being understood by the things that are made, His eternal power and Godhead, so that they are without excuse, because, although they knew God, they did not glorify Him as God, nor were thankful, but became futile in their thoughts, and their foolish hearts were darkened.
>
> Professing to be wise, they became foolish, and changed the glory of the incorruptible God into an image made like corruptible man, birds and four-footed animals and creeping things. Therefore God also gave them up to unclean passions, in the lusts of their hearts, to dishonor their bodies among themselves, who exchanged the truth of God for the lie, and worshiped and served the creature rather than the Creator, who is blessed forever. Amen.
>
> For this reason God gave them up to depraved passions. For even their women exchanged the natural use for what is against nature. Likewise also the men, leaving the natural use of the woman, burned in their lust for one another, men with men committing what is dishonorable, and receiving in them the penalty fitting for their error. (Rom. 1:18-27).

"My word clearly reveals" He continued, "that the rebellion you witnessed was nothing new. The human race had fallen into sin and was in desperate need of redemption. America merely opened itself up to depravity of its own choosing because it rejected Me and the moral protections I had provided. As the Psalmist has written, 'If the foundations are destroyed, what can the righteous do?' (Ps. 11:3).

"My contribution to the sin question was to redeem man from its devastating effects. It was My greatest joy to give My life so that people could be redeemed from sin and cleansed from its destructive power. Homosexual sin is adultery because it is outside of marriage.

"My command is, 'You shall not commit adultery!' I gave this command because I knew the great wreckage that would result from sexual activity outside of marriage."

"But Lord, they redefined marriage to include their sin," I exclaimed.

"They did not understand," Jesus sternly went on, "that I instituted marriage as the earthly counterpart of the heavenly marriage between My bride, the church and Me. My intent was that healthy marriages would present an earthly picture of My eternal marriage to My people.

"Through their redefinition of marriage they touched the dearest thing to My heart. Did I not begin earth's history with a marriage? Did I not begin my earthly ministry at the marriage in Cana? Does not all of earth's history culminate in the marriage of the Christ and His Bride?"

"Marriage was one of those foundational stones that was rejected during that seventy year period, was it not Lord?" I added.

"My Ten Commandments were the moral foundation of America from its beginning: honoring only Me as God, having no idol images of God, honoring My name, remembering the Sabbath day, honoring parents, not murdering, committing adultery, stealing, lying or coveting the possessions of others. I had created the human race and knew what would bring people happiness and fulfillment.

"These laws were a representation of My holy nature. To live by these commandments was to live by the character of the Creator. My laws were not a burden but a protection against the growing onslaught of sin. They rejected Me and thus rejected My character and embraced rebellion and sin. The enemy filled that void with his character and that spelled the collapse of a once great nation."

Failing to fully understand I asked, "Lord, why would a nation reject its own foundational principles?"

Sadly He continued. "They rejected the principles because they wanted to reject Me. They wanted to live their lives without accountability to their Creator. When they were able to dismiss Me and the evidence of My existence, they were able to begin to develop their own principles to live by. In essence they replaced Me with themselves. They became their own gods."

"It sounds like the same deception that was introduced in the Garden of Eden," I put in.

"My adversary" He agreed, "has never really done anything new. His tactic was always to lure people into the lie that they could be like God without submitting to the will of God. Eve ate of the fruit because the serpent convinced her that she "would be like God, knowing good and evil' (Gen.3:5).

"America's leaders and judges made the same mistake. They developed their own definitions of good and evil from the depravity of their own minds. They became their own god and did what was right in their own eyes. The result was one of earth's great tragedies."

"The collapse was devastating to say the least," I agreed.

"America had become so proud and independent of Me that they actually came to believe that their greatness was self-developed. They did not realize that I was behind the success of all aspects of the nation. Economic, cultural, spiritual and international success was a result of My hand upon the nation. As long as they honored Me the country grew and prospered."

I added, "As a teacher I know that they used the school system to introduce many ungodly things into the lives of the young generation."

"Yes," He agreed, "they were able to do these things only by reinterpreting and twisting their own founding document, which I had inspired. I had infused the Constitution with divine principles that would guide the nation morally. It contained provisions for balance in leadership, freedom from tyranny, unalienable human rights, equality, and respect for individual initiative. The document was not perfect but it was man's best effort under God up to that point in history."

"Just as I was finishing high school the judges removed prayer from the schools. From that time it became impossible for schools to use prayer as a guiding influence for the children," I quietly added. "Shortly after that they removed the Bible from schools."

As this conversation with Jesus continued I became amazed at how directly He had been involved in the writing of the Constitution. The founding fathers gathered to compose the words of the great document but Jesus was right there among them guiding them in their noble endeavor. In my own research on this subject I had learned that the founding fathers were almost entirely devout men of God who leaned heavily on the guidance of God.

Benjamin Franklin had made the following famous statement during deliberations at the Constitutional Convention:

> God governs in the affairs of man. And if a sparrow cannot fall to the ground without his notice, is it probable that an empire can rise without His aid? We have been assured in the Sacred Writings that except the Lord build the house, they labor in vain that build it. I firmly believe this. I also believe that, without His concurring aid, we shall succeed in this political building no better than the builders of Babel.

Franklin was prophetic in his understanding that the country would not succeed without the aid of God. Indeed the country would later collapse because subsequent leaders abandoned God and began a Babel project based on human ability.

At one point in the Constitutional Convention the founding fathers had reached a serious deadlock. Franklin stood up and among other things requested that the Convention begin each day in prayer:

> I therefore beg leave to move that henceforth prayers imploring the assistance of Heaven, and its blessings on our deliberations, be held in this Assembly every morning before we proceed to business.

It amazes me to look at such historical statements and then realize that Christ Himself was there among them listening to their pleas and guiding them in their deliberations.

Perceiving my thoughts on this subject the Lord responded, "Yes, I was there among them encouraging them and urging them on by the Spirit. In their frustrations they became willing to commit their deliberations to prayer and My guidance. For this reason the document they finally created was shaped by My inspiration."

I had been a history teacher most of my teaching career, so hearing the Lord talk about how He was with the founding fathers when they were writing the Constitution was a great blessing to me. Having researched the subject I always suspected the influence of Christ on our founding document but now I was hearing it from the mouth of Jesus Himself. My body tingled with excitement.

But then my thoughts turned to the sad reality of the reversal of all that Jesus and the founding fathers had established. After over two hundred years of growth and progress our own court system had systematically reinterpreted the great document in the image of Godless America.

They twisted the words so laboriously chosen by the founding fathers and made them say the opposite of their original meaning. To destroy the founding document was to destroy the foundation upon which the nation was founded. Collapse was inevitable.

As I came out of my thoughts on this subject the Lord was looking deep into the sky at something moving above. He slowly lifted His hand and pointed to a beautiful eagle flying high overhead.

Quietly, as if remembering those early days He said, "That is what I wanted for the people of America—freedom to soar. Human government wants to control people but I wanted them to soar in their individual freedom with the opportunity to reach forward to their destinies. We sought to limit government expression and power so that the people would be free to prosper in Me and in their lives as individuals."

"Lord, I witnessed much of this in my lifetime," I added. "It was sad to see the slow, tragic dismantling of the fabric of our society."

"Sad indeed," the Lord responded. "The country began to do to their Constitution what many of My people were doing to My word, the Bible. Many Christians grew weary of submitting to the simplicity and clarity of My word and began to twist its words for their own convenience.

"This compromise led to homosexual marriage, rampant adultery, the corruption of marriage and family, dishonor of parents and elders, abuse of children, murder of children through abortion, and many other cultural atrocities."

"You had declared that your people were to be the light of the world and the salt of the earth. It seems that during this period the church abandoned its restorative effect on society," I said sadly.

"The truth is they forgot that I said, 'I am the light of the world. He who follows Me shall not walk in darkness, but have the light of life.' (John 8:12). I am the light, and only as people follow Me do they walk in the light and avoid darkness. When My people began to follow religion and their own ingenuity, they stepped out of the light into the darkness as a nation."

At this point the Lord looked past me to a place in His heart and perhaps a place on earth long ago. It is impossible to understand how God can dwell in past, present and future, but I believe there were times when I could see in Jesus' eyes that He was somewhere else in His heart. At this point perhaps He was there in America when the great collapse took place.

And then as if to bring the past into the present conversation He began slowly to recall it for me: "It began when they abandoned Me. When they removed my influence through taking away prayer and My word, immorality of every kind began to break out across the nation. As the morals began to decline, the nation's collective integrity disintegrated. This led to financial and cultural dishonesty.

"This entire breakdown resulted in the people failing to hold their leaders accountable. Leaders then stopped representing the people and began acting on their own behalf. Suddenly the economy began to disintegrate. This led to a domino effect of mini-disasters bringing the country to its knees."

I thought the Lord was finished talking to me about the great collapse of our nation but on the night of March 4 He added details that shook me even further. I can only assume that the Lord wants to warn people in the twenty-first century so that those who have ears to hear can prepare their hearts for what is to come. I was stunned by what I learned.

The west will experience a protracted drought that will seriously curtail the water supply. Agriculture in the Central Valley will be limited for several years resulting in high food prices and shortages. During the great Dust Bowl of the thirties the Midwest experienced the drought and people migrated to the west seeking work.

During this drought people will be leaving California and move to the Midwest and other areas in search of a livelihood. This migration will create a cultural transformation in the west as immigrants from an overwhelmed southern border move in mass out of violence and corruption in Mexico into California. This will contribute to the overwhelming of the economy of the state, thus sparking the collapse.

The southern borders of the United States from California to Texas will erupt into violent clashes as drug lords and criminal elements move north. The cities of the border areas will be overrun with outside influences creating fear and intimidation. The school system will be virtually shut down by this violence and so many families, especially Christians, will migrate north in search of stability. The National Guard and federal troops will be sent in to try to keep the peace but this will only add to the chaos in the southern border states.

Los Angeles will experience a heavy earthquake during major traffic hours that will kill thousands. The freeway system will be shut down seriously limiting commerce in and out of the city. Of course this will have a serious effect on the economy of the state and nation.

San Francisco, where one would think there would be a serious earthquake, instead experiences a cultural earthquake as the city collapses from its own economic policies. The city becomes a haven for homeless people who move there from throughout the state and country in search of welfare help. Prostitution, drug abuse, gangs, and crime explode in the city causing a collapse of the city's economy. The National Guard and specially trained police will be sent in to provide security.

The federal government, in the wake of this collapse, will declare a form of martial law across the country. It will seize control of National Guards in many states and will bring troops home from oversees to provide security in a nation in chaos.

The central government will have virtual dictatorial control of the nation. For the most part, the country will be ruled from the east coast as the big cities of Washington D.C., New York, Chicago, Philadelphia, and Atlanta become command centers for the federal government. Federal elections will be suspended indefinitely as the government seizes control in the name of national security.

Christians will be blamed for this collapse. They will be criticized for their lack of openness to diversity because of their stand regarding homosexuality and other religions. They will be condemned for choosing homeschooling over the government school system and for insisting on parental rights over government intrusion.

Gathering in homes will be outlawed in many city communities and any kind of public displays of Christian messages will be banned or limited. Gradually, the church will be driven underground into informal gatherings in secret places throughout the country.

The final result will be a nation brought to its knees. Two things will then begin to take place. First, a strong, vibrant, living, church will quietly grow and prosper in the underground environment caused by the collapse. The rising up of the church will begin in earnest, setting the stage for the great end time expression of the full grown, empowered, body of Christ, the bride of Christ.

Secondly, a nation on its knees will gradually experience restoration and stand to its feet in a form calculated for the latter days.

† Chapter 12: The Rising Up of the Church

Even before the collapse of America I began to see a very slow but real emerging of a different form of church life. At first it was so gradual that many did not notice. Most Christians were looking for some kind of revival that would come sweeping over the horizon and arrive in a tidal wave of power.

But this revival was like a slowly rising tide that was only noticed by those looking for it. It was originating in dry, hungry hearts yearning for the presence of the Lord. Instead of coming over the horizon this revival was flowing gently from the hearts of the people.

Jesus had declared, "Whoever believes in Me, as the Scriptures have said, out of his heart shall flow rivers of living water" (John 7:38). This slowly developing renewal was not coming from external religious influence but from the hungry hearts of people desperate for Christ. Revival always begins in the heart of man and from it flows.

I asked the Lord about this: "Jesus, why is it that revivals seem to burst forth from nowhere and sweep onto the scene with spiritual passion?"

His reply was simple but pregnant with truth, "Hungry people seek Me. When people seek Me, I meet them where they are and sit with them like I'm sitting with you now. Did I not say, 'Seek and you will find?' My presence brings revival—nothing else will do."

His searching eyes scanned the horizon of our heavenly vista as He let the next words flow out with tender compassion: "I met the Samaritan woman at the well. There she found the living waters she had sought. Zacchaeus sought Me in his sycamore tree and I met him at his house for a meal and a conversation. His life was changed. I met Lazarus' seeking family in their living room and often we ate together.

"Matthew and his family received Me into their home and his hunger was satisfied as we fellowshipped around a meal. I met the Pharisee Nicodemus in the cover of night but his seeking heart was soon uncovered as we spoke of new life in the Spirit. I met My disciples on the beach of the sea and we had breakfast from the bounty of My fish blessing."

Jesus paused for a moment and gently reached out His hand to touch my shoulder and said, "And I met you at your bedside that night in 1963 when we spoke face to face for the first time. In that moment of seeking, you quietly entered My presence and My kingdom."

We both took a moment to remember and bask in the goodness of that special day. I was remembering the freedom I experienced in my spirit and no doubt the Lord was remembering the joy of a new child in His kingdom. We didn't move quickly from this moment but smiled and looked at each other with quiet satisfaction.

I was especially quiet when I responded, "Master, I see so clearly now that there were times in my life when I made a serious mistake in my thinking."

"And what was that mistake that troubles you so," He asked.

"I fell for the notion that spiritual restoration comes from principles, and programs, and human manipulation. I didn't see the simplest truth—that your presence is the key to all spiritual life. I sought ways to bring revival but did not seek you—the Way," I said with some awkwardness.

I paused for a moment as I gathered my thoughts and began again, "The rising up of the church arrived because people became so hungry that they threw aside the programs of men and began to seek you. They became so hungry that nothing but your presence could satisfy them."

"It has always been so that I do My best work when people are desperate for life—when they reach the bottom of their lives and have nowhere to look but up. I meet them there and touch their desperate lives with My presence.

"Out of such desperation the rising up of the church took place. A slow rising of the spiritual tide occurred as people left the confines of religion and found their way into My life-changing presence."

"And that must be why you call this time period 'the rising up of the church.' The church had reached such a low place of hunger and despair that they could only rise up in your life and power," I put in.

"Yes, indeed, My son. And that was the humble but real beginning of changes that would shake heaven and earth for My kingdom."

I now see that the rising up of the church coincides with the collapse of our country. Christians in America had not known hardship since the great struggle to establish the nation and get it onto a stable footing. It survived the Civil War and the two world wars and the Great Depression because of this stable foundation.

In recent years the country has abandoned its foundational mores, resulting in the predictable fall of the Republic. As financial, social, political, and spiritual unrest spread through the country the church was forced to rise up.

Countries like China have long since discovered a monumental truth—troublesome times cause the church to come together in unity and love resulting in the release of God's power in signs and wonders. The church in America will experience this during the collapse of the country they have put their trust in for so many years.

"Lord," I asked, "What was it like for the church during those troubling days?"

The Lord bowed His head and rested it in His right hand with His eyes closed as He considered His answer. He was not quick to answer but quietly pondered this question very carefully.

"Many of My people," He began, "were ready for this collapse because they were listening to My Spirit, who prepared them for the collapse. They were not caught off guard because they were prepared physically and spiritually for the event. Many Christians had already begun meeting in homes in the simple way that I have purposed. They had learned to assimilate My word into their lives through fellowship and prayer. They had learned to allow Me to be the guest of honor in their gatherings. The practicality of body life was instrumental in helping them to be prepared for the collapse.

"On the other hand," the Lord continued, "many in the organized church were caught off guard. They were unprepared physically or spiritually because they were involved in organizations that did not emphasize the word, fellowship and hearing My voice. They became passive in their approach to the faith. This complacency caused them to be caught off guard like soldiers on furlough. Many abandoned the faith because the trials of the day were too much for their meager faith. A great falling away from the faith came to pass."

The Lord was making the case that those who had listened to His voice during the time leading up to the collapse were prepared. They had abandoned just going to church and had learned to be the church through the practical simplicity of the body of Christ.

I wondered how it was for those who were true followers of Christ. So I asked the Lord, "Jesus how were the true followers of Christ affected by the collapse?"

"It was the worst of times and the best of times for My followers in America," replied the Lord. "They were hit with persecution and troubles the country has never experienced up to that point. Many lost their jobs and homes and were left without a means of livelihood. Large churches closed for lack of support. The government began to oppose organized Christianity through taxation, and other political pressures. Christians were arrested in some cases for openly practicing their faith. The church was driven underground."

I felt a foreboding sense of alarm as Jesus finished His reply. It is one thing to be sitting around with some Christian friends talking about what may happen in the future but it is quite different when Jesus speaks about it—especially when He is speaking in the past tense. His words come with finality and certainty. When He speaks, the truth is openly revealed. The only thing remaining is our response to what He says. My heart was troubled for the church as I realized what it was to face.

Of course the Lord sensed this anxiety on my part. "Don't be alarmed," He said. "This is all part of My plan. I did not cause the collapse of America but I was there to use it for the benefit of My people. My church rose up out of the rubble of this collapse. They came together out of necessity to help and support one another. They tore down the fences of separation they had built and came together solely for one another and for My purpose."

My anxiety turned to excitement as the Lord spoke of this positive result of the collapse. I could see how God would step in to cause things to work together for good. He would use the collapse of the country and the hardships it would bring to stir up the church to love and good works.

"What form did the church take during these difficult times?" I asked the Lord.

"The church grew and was shaped by My Spirit," He replied. "In some cases large vacated church buildings were taken over by a group of families who lived together communally. Those who were working brought home their paychecks and shared with those who were not able to work. Those staying at home cultivated a garden and raised chickens for food. They gathered regularly as the church to build one another up spiritually and to honor Me. This ministry of the saints caused the church to grow."

Jesus was shaking His head in the affirmative as He made this last statement. He was obviously pleased by what He knew would take place during those troubled days. He knew that the trials His followers faced would produce in them "an exceedingly abundant and eternal weight of glory" as Paul put it (2 Cor. 4:17).

He knew that the testing of their faith produced endurance and that endurance caused them to grow toward spiritual completeness in God. For this reason James had told us to "Count it all joy, my brothers, when you encounter various trials" (James 1:2). James knew that God's best is released in His people when trials come.

Jesus seemed excited to tell another success story. After a pause He continued. "In large cities Christians gathered in homes throughout the city. When local governments shut them down they simply gathered somewhere else as the Spirit directed.

"In these informal gatherings they shared everything they had, spirit, soul and body. There were no needs among them because each believer shared what they had with their brothers and sisters. People of their communities were drawn into these fellowships out of the desperation of the times. The church grew by multiplication throughout the cities and in the countryside."

Jesus was truly on a roll now as He triumphantly recounted how the church rose up during the collapse. He was excited for His church and the way she responded when troubles came. Nothing could make Him happier then to see His children coming together in love and unity through His Spirit.

"Many Christians migrated to various places in the country out of necessity," the Lord continued. "They did not move to areas based solely on financial needs but were looking for other believers and the opportunity to gather with them. All across the country Christians gathered with one another not based on religious compulsion or tradition but out of genuine desire to be together. They gradually returned to the simplicity of fellowship I always intended for them. The result was a vibrant, growing, powerful church throughout the country."

In many ways Christians in America in the twenty-first century are spoiled. Somehow we have bought into the notion that we can have the fullness of what God has to offer without paying the price of commitment. Some Christians erroneously believe that God's grace means that there is never any price to be paid to be a follower of Christ.

Jesus said, "If anyone would come after Me let him deny himself, take up his cross and follow Me" (Matt. 16:24). There is no price to be paid for our justification in Christ, but there is a price to be paid to be a true follower of Christ. The price we must pay is our lives. We must deny ourselves to follow Him. We must take up a cross to go to the death of our self in order to be His followers.

Paul said, "Indeed, all who desire to live a godly life in Christ Jesus will be persecuted" (2 Tim. 3:12). Living a truly godly life stirs up the enemy and his workers of destruction. In America we have chosen the pathway of least resistance. We have decided to be casual Christians, go to church once a week, all the while expecting a life of blessing. We are spoiled and not prepared to fight the good fight of faith.

There is a time approaching, perhaps sooner than we think, when all of this will change. Listen to the Holy Spirit for directions so you will not be caught off guard. Let Him show you how to be prepared physically and spiritually. Find a setting where real body life is practiced. Let life within His body, the church, build you up and prepare you for the coming collapse. Let the church be a haven of protection from the complacency of the age. Get ready for the collapse that leads to the rising up of the church, the body of Christ.

† Chapter 13: I will Build My Church

Christians have a hard time seeing the ultimate victory of the church because they have a distorted idea of what the true church is. To most people the church is a building they go to on Sundays to sit passively while a prepared program is presented. There is little participation on the part of the members of the body of Christ, and generally one man dominates what is said and done in the gathering. Christ is mentioned throughout the meeting in the songs and prayers but somehow He is relegated to a secondary place while others assume the place of honor.

Through my conversations with the Lord at the mercy seat I now know that even in the early twenty-first century the organized church is beginning to die. Most people do not perceive this but it is true nonetheless. Recent decades of moral decay in family and marriage have produced a generation of wounded people who are seeking answers to their brokenness. For the most part they are not finding the answers in the organized church which is not structured to meet these needs. They are leaving in droves.

Satan had tried to destroy a generation of people through abortion, murder, child abuse, sexual depravity, disease and social unrest. His tactics on the exterior seemed to be working but on the other hand they had created a desperate generation of hungry people seeking for an answer to the spiritual vacuum in their lives. Ironically, the enemy of God helped to set the stage for massive changes that would come to the church.

When I began to ask the Lord about my concerns for the organized church I had an idea how He felt about it but I had never heard it from His own mouth. During one of our nighttime conversations I broached the subject.

I spoke out of my deep concern: "Lord, the organized church during most of my life seemed to be a mere religious machine that existed for its own purpose. The machine seemed to roll along oblivious to the real healing needs of the people."

Tenderly, the Lord began saying, "I love My people. They are My sheep and I am the Good Shepherd. During most of your lifetime false shepherds, some of whom were well meaning, used My sheep for their own purposes and power. They erroneously took My sheep out of My fold and built new fences in which to corral and control them. They did not feed them properly nor lead them to the living water. They used the sheep to feed themselves and construct large buildings and programs they referred to as 'ministries' and generally neglected their spiritual health."

"It seemed to me at the time, Lord that Christian leaders honored the word of God in matters dealing with the individual walk but failed to see the Bible's clear teachings about the corporate arrangement of your church."

With concern in His voice the Lord agreed: "They neglected My words about the corporate composition of My church because it ran counter to the plans they had devised. They wanted the shape of the church to reflect their own vision instead of My eternal purpose. Instead of listening to Me for direction, they sought direction through expediency and practicality. If it worked for their vision they did it regardless of how I felt about it."

But then the Lord used those words that I had heard Him speak several times in our night time conversations. He leaned toward me and with that special twinkle in His eyes He said, "But it wasn't like that in the latter days was it?"

I took that to mean that in the latter days the church reaches a place of spiritual unity, love and power and completes its destiny as the conquering bride at the marriage of the Lamb. The present condition of the church, in His words, is not the final word.

This present expression of the church does not fulfill the declaration of Jesus to His disciples, "I will build My church and the gates of hell shall not prevail against it" (Matt. 16:18). The God of peace does crush Satan under the feet of His church (Rom. 16:20). The Seed of Eve, Christ expressed in His spiritual offspring the church, does bruise the head of the serpent in fulfillment of God's Garden of Eden prophecy.

Then the Lord picked up on His statement about the latter days: "Many who have read My word have missed the point that all of My individual encounters with hungry people were aimed at producing My corporate body. When I met with the Samaritan women at Jacob's well, the whole city was touched. When I met with seeking people in their homes the whole family was changed by My presence."

The Lord paused for a moment as if remembering a special moment and then He continued, "When Peter received the revelation that I am the Christ, My immediate declaration was 'Upon this rock I will build My church' (Matt. 16:18). My aim is not to enlighten individuals merely for personal knowledge but to produce My body, the church.

"When the multitudes surrounded Me I was not impressed with the crowds but sought quiet moments with My disciples when I could build within them a sense of My corporate purpose. I was pursuing a body, not just many spiritual individuals."

"So throughout your earthly ministry you were preparing your disciples to be the body of Christ," I commented.

"Yes, this is a truth missed by many. Most Christians believe that the church had its beginning on the Day of Pentecost when I poured out My Holy Spirit. The truth is the church began when I first called Simon and Andrew to follow Me. I said, 'Follow Me and I will make you fishers of men.' (Matt. 4:19). They followed Me and became the church.

"The church exists when I am in the midst of two or three who are together for My purpose. I called Simon and Andrew not just to be devout followers, but to catch their generation in the net of My eternal purpose. They accepted the challenge and the rest is glorious history."

This prompted a question I had always had so I ventured out, "Lord, I've always wondered why there were only one hundred and twenty disciples in the upper room waiting for your promise of the Spirit. You had touched the lives of so many and yet in this room such a small group had responded."

"Your question makes My point. I never gave myself fully to the multitudes that followed Me. I gave Myself to those who met Me face to face and listened to My words. Of course there were others in the city waiting with this small group, but this band of believers represented the remnant of those whose lives I had touched. They were there in that upper room totally committed to Me and what I would do on their behalf. They were not disappointed."

Even as I write these words I am completely astounded at the way the body of Christ has risen up around us in our time of need. My hope for the church has been renewed by two things: Christ's words to me and the love expressed to us by the saints.

Many of you have been part of this great testimony of love in the body of Christ. You have come to fill our wood bin with wood and carry wood and kindling into the house. You have brought us food on many occasions including chicken soup, lamb steaks, enchiladas and chocolate chip cookies. One dear sister sent us a card with a scripture verse every day for two months. What a blessing! Many of you have visited us and stayed for heartfelt fellowship and given us gifts of encouragement. Some visited us in the hospital and fellowshipped and prayed with us there.

You have driven me to town for my many doctor's appointments and blood tests. You have sent us cards and other encouraging letters and emails. Some have left money to help with expenses. Others gathered with us on two occasions to pray as we entered the next chemo-therapy treatment. You laid hands on me and prayed God's perfect will for my life.

All of you have prayed for us as the Lord directed. One dear person allowed us use of his RV so Mary would have a place to stay close to the hospital. Many of you gave into a fund to help us purchase helpful nutritional supplements. One dear brother fixed my shower so I could take my shower while sitting and attached a bar so I could exit easier and he fixed our screen door.

You have pruned our grape vines and Mary's roses. You have raked our leaves and cleaned our yard. You have mowed our lawn and helped with fixing the lawn mower. You walked our dog daily when I was too weak. You have spent hours cleaning our house when Mary was my caregiver. I have received dozens of encouraging phone calls. One friend took the time to come to the house on more than one occasion to show historical slides and just spend time with me. A dear brother sent out regular updates on our condition by email.

Some have quoted uplifting scripture and sung songs of comfort. Some of you came from many miles away to visit us and encourage us when we were homebound. You sprayed the trails on our property with Roundup to kill the weeds. When our vacuum cleaner broke down you brought us a new one. I have received hugs and kisses from so many of you along the way as you tenderly expressed your love. Our children supported us through prayer, visits, and acts of kindness.

All of this and more you did because you loved us and showed that love through acts of kindness. You sacrificed your time to let the Lord bless us through you. Thank you for your acts of love and your prayers. We will never forget the love you showed us in our time of need. I can truthfully say that all of the suffering has been worthwhile because it allowed me to see and experience your love.

Through this ordeal not one person has come to us like one of Job's counselors to preach to us about why we are suffering. Not one negative, judgmental word was spoken but many constructive words of wisdom were given to us. Thank you for your obedience.

Truly, the body of Christ is beautiful and you have expressed that beauty before our very eyes. My hope for a rising church is renewed.

† Chapter 14: A New Wineskin

I know for a certainty that the church of the latter days will not resemble what we see today. Change in its practical expression is underway even as I write these words. God has prepared a new wine for the last days of planet earth, however many those days may be.

That wine of His presence cannot be poured into the dried up wineskin of the building-oriented approach to the church with its one man professional ministry and gross neglect of the needs of the saints and the body of Christ. Jesus has a better idea. We talked about it and what follows is the wondrous outcome of that conversation.

The Lord's eyes sparkled with divine enthusiasm as He spoke of His earthly ministry with the ones He had chosen to follow Him: "I chose men to be more than My followers. I was looking for those whose hearts would embrace the commitment to be My beloved bride, the body of Christ fully expressed on earth.

"I prepared each of their lives to be wineskins that I would fill with the new wine of My life-giving Spirit. But My ultimate goal was to prepare among them a corporate spiritual body that would live in love, unity, and power as a testimony to the world of My love and grace. This body was to grow and mature to reach a place of commitment described by Paul as 'the unity of the faith and of the knowledge of the Son of God, to a perfect man, to the measure of the stature of the fullness of Christ'" (Eph. 4: 13).

"The fourth chapter of Ephesians," I volunteered, "became very special to me over the years of my life. I saw in it a clear presentation of your perfect will for your church. The chapter seemed to break down the process you would use in the age of the church to bring your people to a unified, loving, corporate expression of your spiritual body."

Jesus continued, "I put the revelation of My eternal purpose into Paul's heart and he was faithful to proclaim it and write it in My word. He suffered much to see the beginning of its fulfillment in his lifetime. Through his sufferings he learned that My strength in Him was made perfect in weakness. In this strength he helped conquer the first century with My message. His words set the tone and released the power for the great victory of the church that came in the latter days."

Jesus paused for a moment, no doubt reflecting on His great love for Paul. I too had learned to love Paul through His powerful words that set forth the way of salvation and the revelation of the church, the body of Christ.

As Jesus soaked in that moment I volunteered a question: "Lord it seemed that on the Day of Pentecost when you poured out your Spirit on the disciples that everything just fell into place. It seemed that nothing could ever stop the church."

"My remnant of one hundred and twenty, who waited for My promise in that upper room, had become a wineskin into which I could pour My new wine. They had faithfully fulfilled My statement, 'Where two or three are gathered together in My name, there I am in the midst of them.' (Matt. 18: 20). They were not only faithful individual followers but were in one accord, devoting themselves to prayer as they waited. They were a corporate wineskin waiting to be filled."

I broke out excitedly, "And filled they were on that glorious day! I wish that I could have been there to see it."

"It was a wonderful day," the Lord continued. "But many have missed what really happened on that day. I was not just filling many individual wineskins but also one corporate wineskin, My precious body, My fullness upon the earth."

"Lord, was the manifestation of speaking in other tongues significant to this corporate body you were creating?" I wondered out loud.

"My message in the explosion of speaking in unknown languages was that this body I was creating was for all the ethnic peoples of earth. My mission was for the body of Christ to reach beyond racial, gender, and social barriers to produce a body unified not by fleshly characteristics but by My indwelling life."

"Your word says there were people from many different nations who had come to Jerusalem for the celebration," I put in.

"My message to them through my gifts of their languages was that they were included in what I was doing. They were to be part of the body I was creating and they would be privileged to take word of it back to their homes."

"And then the new wineskin began to form and express itself," I responded. "A corporate shape began to emerge as the disciples sought together for the way to gather and express your life."

The Lord then clarified what I said. "Actually, the disciples merely continued to do what we had been doing together for three and a half years. They began to meet with one another with me as the guest of honor. Now, I was among them in the Spirit and our times of companionship continued in their gatherings."

The Lord paused for a moment and then turned to His word: "'And they continually devoted themselves to the apostles' teaching and to the fellowship, to the breaking of bread and prayers' (Acts 2: 42). These words reveal the simplicity of body life to which I called them."

"It seemed simple and yet I know in your wisdom the wineskin you were creating was very significant for the age of the church," I responded.

"The words of this verse contain a parable explaining how the body of Christ is to function," He began to explain. "Every physical body needs food for its growth. The food must be assimilated into the body through the coordinated working of the systems of the body. The digestive, circulatory, respiratory, muscular and other systems work together to get the food to every cell of the body. This results in the healthy growth of the body."

He paused to let this all sink into my thinking. Then He took up where He left off. "My spiritual body has the same needs. The food for the body of Christ is referred to here as the apostles' teaching. My word is the bread of life, the food supply for the body of Christ.

"Fellowship is the spiritual equivalent to the working together of the systems of the physical body. As each member shares with the others the spiritual food of the word is broken down, digested and taken into the various parts of the body. Fellowship is the sharing of My life-giving nutrients through active participation of the members of the body of Christ. As they share through prayer, testimony, gifts, songs, lessons and other means of participation, the whole body is built up."

"Lord, how would the prayers mentioned in this verse tie in to this body parable?" I asked.

"The body must always be in subjection to and communicate with the head. I am the Head of the body of Christ and the prayers are the means by which that communication takes place. The church is My body. It is to express My will and purpose and move according to My guidance. This happens through the regular, continuing prayers of the members. Prayer is like the nervous system of the body in that it allows communication between the head and the rest of the body."

"Wow!" I exclaimed. "What a clear parable of how the new wineskin was to come together in the early church! Fellowship and prayers are so crucial to the healthy growth of the body of Christ."

But there was one more part of the verse that I was curious about. "Jesus, what was the significance of the 'breaking of bread' mentioned in this passage?"

"During My earthly ministry with the disciples, we often ate together. During these meals we had our sit-down talks that changed their lives and readied them for what was to come. The family meal is the place where people turn their attention to one another. There is conversation, and laughter, songs and sharing of hearts.

"When Matthew chose to follow me I met with him that evening in his home with His sinning tax collector friends. Many of them were set free through our informal time together. The eyes of the Emmaus disciples were opened when we sat down to meal together. I had breakfast of fish with the disciples at the seashore while they mended their nets from the abundant catch of the day. We ate physical food but it was the spiritual bread of life we enjoyed the most."

Jesus seemed to rise up in His seat as He readied Himself for His next statement. Slowly that wonderful smile came across His face and He continued. "It was My last meal with them that set the tone for this new wineskin for the church age. At that meal I gave My church for all generations a gift by which to remember Me. It was My engagement ring to My bride."

"I broke the bread and said, 'Take and eat. This is My body which is broken for you. Do this in remembrance of Me.' Then I gave them the cup and said, 'This cup is the New Covenant in My blood. As often as you do this do it in remembrance of Me.'

"At each gathering of the saints in the early church the Lord's Supper was always present. It showed that I was the guest of honor in all of their gatherings. I was with them in Spirit and the communion meal was their way of remembering Me and the time when I would drink of it again with My glorified bride in the kingdom."

I sat amazed at how clearly the Lord had explained how the wineskin of the church was able to contain the new wine of the Spirit. It became clear to me why the word says, "Then fear came upon every soul, and many wonders and signs were done through the apostles" (Acts 2: 43). This great reverence for God and the signs and wonders were the direct result of the body gathering in love and oneness with Christ as the guest of honor.

The same passage of scripture says, "So continuing daily with one accord in the temple, and breaking bread from house to house, they ate their food with gladness and simplicity of heart, praising God and having favor with all the people. And the Lord added to the church daily those who were being saved" (Acts 2: 46, 47).

It is clear that the body of Christ functioning as Christ had designed it was having an incredible impact on the city. The Holy Spirit was not only upon them in power, and in them as spiritual life, but was spreading out among the people as the church ate their meals together with joyous hearts, praising God. The church was growing and prospering through the simplest and most enjoyable way imaginable. What an incredible wineskin the Lord had fashioned!

It was amazing to me that even though there was still only one church in the city the saints met in homes in small groups. From the numbers mentioned in Acts, the church had grown into the thousands in a short time and yet they continued to gather throughout the city in homes. Instead of isolating themselves in big worship buildings they saturated the city with the life of God, mingling with the people.

The church was doing what Jesus always did—it moved among the people to minister His life-giving presence. Occasionally they gathered at the temple for big celebrations but mostly they met informally around meals in one another's homes.

Paul explains in several places how they gathered. Of course there was always the Lord's Supper with Christ as the guest of honor. The physical meal and the spiritual meal were shared food. Everyone brought a song, a lesson, an expression of a gift of the Spirit, a prophecy, a revelation or just an excited testimony, along with a gift of food (Eph. 5:18-21; 1 Cor. 14; Col. 3:16, 17; Acts 2:42-47).

They sang songs together and made melody in their hearts to the Lord. Through this open, free participation the food of the word was assimilated into the body and it was continually built up and strengthened. Paul said, "Let all things be done for edification" (1 Cor. 14:26). The individual and corporate building up of the church was the aim of every gathering.

Finally, I could no longer contain my excitement at this clear picture of the simple way of church expression the Lord had created. I could see clearly that He had patterned it after His own spiritual temperament. The gatherings of the saints were a continuation of His earthly ministry, except now He met with them through the Spirit.

"Lord," I burst out, "It seems that through the church you were having even more of an impact then during your earthly ministry!"

"That was My intention, of course. Had I not promised the disciples, 'Truly, truly, I say to you, he who believes in Me, the works that I do he will do also, and greater works than these he will do, because I go to My Father'? (John 14:12). When I went to My Father with My finished work of atonement, He sent to My church the Advocate, the Holy Spirit in My name. Through Him the church continued in power with My blessing and presence. The works accomplished in a short time were greater than even the works I had done."

I sat amazed at the wisdom of the Lord. As I contemplated these simple truths I wondered how the later organized church could have missed the amazing simplicity of God's plan. But that would be another conversation with the Master.

† Chapter 15: Drifting Away from Simplicity

Even in my excitement concerning the explosion of the early church, there was a nagging question I needed to ask the Lord. I had some historical knowledge concerning how the church drifted from this early simplicity, but I wanted to hear it from Him.

"Lord," I inquired, "how did the church eventually move away from this amazingly effective wineskin you had fashioned?"

The Lord was quick to answer as if anticipating my question, "They did wonderfully well for two centuries. My word spread throughout much of the world. Churches spread throughout the cities of the known world. My apostles and many others gave their lives taking the gospel to nations and peoples far away. It was a glorious beginning!"

At this point I could see an obvious sadness spread over the face of my Lord. His eyes lifted to some place far away in time and space. He began slowly but deliberately: "They began to make two big mistakes. The first error was allowing one man to take control of the local church. I inspired My apostles to choose plural groups of mature men to lead the local churches. They were older men—elders whose character had been tested so that they could oversee the flock of God without selfish motives. One man in control always leads to disorder and imbalance because the self nature will usually win out when a person is given power."

I responded, "Lord was that the error of Diotrephes in John's third letter?"

"Yes, Diotrephes wanted to have the number one position in one of the churches overseen by John (3 John 9). Also, he was rejecting the apostolic helpers being sent from John to help the church.

"This is another tragedy of one-person leadership. For want of power over the people, the lone leader often rejects the ministries of the five equipping gifts I gave to the church. When the apostles, prophets, evangelists, pastors and teachers are rejected, the process of equipping the saints breaks down."

"It seems that for most of my Christian life all I knew of leadership in the church was the one-man pastor form. I also saw that the equipping ministries were noticeably absent," I said.

The Lord was quick to respond: "Paul laid out my plan for the church in the fourth chapter of Ephesians. After My ascension I gave the five equipping ministries to the church (4:11). Each of these five gifts is especially anointed by My Spirit to equip the saints for their own ministries to the church. Everyone has a part and the equipping ministries help restore people from the ravages of the world and then equip them to function effectively as members of My body (4:12). The elders are the overseers and leaders of the local church but the five-fold equippers are stationed within the body to equip the saints through My leading."

Remembering Ephesians chapter four fondly I excitedly said, "And as I remember it the proper functioning of these equippers results in the saints serving one another effectively leading, of course, to the building up of the church. The end result is 'We all come to the unity of the faith and of the knowledge of the Son of God, to a full grown man, to the measure of the stature of the fullness of Christ' (4: 13).

"Yes, the goal of the wineskin I created has always been the complete maturity of My body. The measure of its maturity is when it becomes, according to Paul's words, 'The fullness of Him who fills all in all' (Eph. 1: 23). The body is My bride. She is destined to be full grown to the 'measure of the stature of the fullness of Christ.' The latter days will see the complete fulfillment of this destiny."

I tried to bring all of this together in my mind with a question: "So, Lord, your design for leadership in the church was a group of mature men who lead the church through their own example of faith and obedience? And you gave supernaturally inspired gifts of people to the church to work among the saints equipping them for ministry? You never intended for one person to be the sole leader of the local church?"

Jesus was shaking His head in the affirmative but I could tell He had a deep concern. He slowly began to express it saying, "Eventually some began to be moved by fear. Their fear of rising heresies and worldly challenges caused some leaders to consolidate power in one person. At first they elevated one of the elders to the position of lead elder.

"Eventually, they began to separate elders from bishops and the bishop became the sole leader of the local church with the elders under him. This was the beginning of the one-man form of church leadership that would lead to serious spiritual decline in My church."

"Lord," I broke in. "It seems to me that would have taken away from the participatory fellowship that you had established by the Spirit in the church gatherings. If one person began to take control of the ministry of the church it seems that the believers would drift into passivity."

"And that is exactly what began to happen," He responded. "My elders were chosen to be leaders because My people are followers. They need righteous shepherds who have no ulterior motives. As selfish motives began to develop in the hearts of the leaders the sheep slowly abandoned their places of service to those in control.

"When the saints stop sharing in the dynamic of fellowship, the church is not being built up and spiritual decline sets in. This was the tragedy of the third century of the church age."

After a pause He continued. "The consolidation of this power continued through the centuries until the entire ministry of the saints was replaced by professional clergy. The church grew as a political power in the world but lost its vitality as a spiritual force in the world. My word became secondary to the word of self-proclaimed experts.

"My life was replaced by programs initiated by men. The church, My people, were now sheep in a fold constructed by men. It gives Me great sadness to say that controlling men stole My sheep and began to use them for their own selfish motives."

"Lord, you spoke of a second big mistake that also contributed to the gradual drifting from your simple plan for the church," I said.

With a shaking of His head and a grimace on His face Jesus replied, "The second big mistake was moving from the informality of home gatherings and concentrating the ministry of the churches in buildings. Special buildings were the natural outgrowth of the one-man form of leadership that developed. Consolidating of power meant corralling My people into centers where they could be controlled.

"Eventually, the church was seen as a religious program connected to a building in the city. Gone were the gatherings in homes with Me as the guest of honor. Gone was the excitement in the cities as the church mingled with the people and brought My life to them. Now the people were separated away in buildings for the sake of controlling men."

I joined the Lord's dismay over this development of history. "Lord, you intended it to be so simple and yet men complicated it with their man-made programs. I must confess that I participated in this for much of my life."

The Lord's face lit up as He turned the conversation in a more cheerful direction. Confidently, He said, "But the destiny I called forth in My church, My bride, would not be crushed. She was destined to rise from the ashes of defeat into the glorious victory of the latter days. My church would eventually return to its humble roots—to the informality of the home and the comfort of leadership by mature elders. My church would rise in victory because My word cannot be broken!"

This glorious declaration from the Lord brought this conversation to an upbeat ending that encouraged me greatly. The Lord has a way of seeing through the confusion caused by men into the realm of eternity. There He sees the ultimate triumph of His life expressed in His people. I could not help but join in His optimism for His eternal purpose.

† Chapter 16: Love: The Manifestation of God

Love. One cannot be in the presence of Jesus long without becoming aware that He is love manifest. Love is expressed in every word, every smile, every twinkle in His eye. Even words of correction and sternness are somehow shaped by His love. I wanted to know more about His nature of love for I want more and more to be a person who walks in His perfect love.

"Lord," I asked, "Your word says that God is love (1 John 4:8). I have always thought of love as an emotional expression of the soul. How is it that you are love in the sense of this verse?"

Jesus smiled that smile that gave away His delight with my question. He shook His head in agreement with my concern. His answer surprised me at first: "Love is more than an emotion. He is a person—God. Real love can only be known in God. It is My nature and everything I do is motivated by its transforming power."

"Lord, I know that when I am in your presence I am overwhelmed by the love that seems to surround you," I volunteered. "Your loves pulls me into close fellowship with you. Your love is infectious."

"I wish that I could infect the whole human race with My love," He responded. "Love is the most powerful force in the universe. My enemy has bet his eternal state on the notion that his evil will win out in the end. He underestimates love. It cannot fail and cannot be overcome."

"People throw the word love around too loosely," I said. "It seems we really don't understand it much."

Jesus smiled and nodded His head, knowing the flippancy of man toward His greatest gift to them. But His words showed He understood: "Love cannot be known apart from Me. Man has manufactured his own kind of soulish love, but this is a poor substitute for the real thing. The love that emanates from the unredeemed soul of man is tainted with selfishness and human weakness. Godly love always puts self last and others first. Love is supernatural—it is not a natural quality of man but one that must come from God."

"Since love is the expression of your nature, Lord, it would seem to be the highest state one can experience," I said, trying to grasp love's greatness.

"Love is the greatest spiritual fruit," He continued. "It grows in the lives of those who become My true followers. Love is the product of the transformed soul. Once the soul is denied and crucified I begin the process of transforming your mind, emotions, and will and love begins to grow in your heart. In this love My people can actually begin to act like God and reflect His nature. Love is God manifest."

"In your word it says that a scribe once asked you to identify the most important commandment. I remember you spoke to him of love."

Jesus replied, "There is no greater commandment than to love. I told the scribe, 'You shall love the Lord your God with all your heart, with all your soul, and with all your mind. And the second is like it. You shall love your neighbor as yourself' (Matt. 22:37, 39). Of course people often miss My key word 'all.' To fulfill this commandment is to love God with all of your heart, soul, and mind not with just a portion. Love must fill all the empty places of your heart replacing the natural selfishness you were born with. This is My ultimate desire for all My followers."

I was somewhat startled by the Lord's strong explanation. It seemed to me at first hearing that such a state of love is almost unattainable. I was contemplating this when the Lord continued.

"I want your whole heart. I am not satisfied with just a portion. Love must invade every compartment of your innermost being so that you are wholly mine and wholly enveloped in love. This love for Me will be reflected in the same love for your neighbor. I said that the second commandment is 'like the first.' By this I meant that the love you have for God is expressed toward the people in your life. To love God is to love His children. The person who says he loves God but does not love others is sadly mistaken. Love does not pick and choose. It freely flows out of a pure heart."

At this point I was overwhelmed with the thought that I have fallen far short of God's standard of true love. I talk much about it and have embraced it as a doctrine for my life but hearing the words of the God, who is love, made me realize how limited my love has been. I wanted the Lord to know how I felt.

"Lord," I pleaded, "How can I have such love?"

"My servant John wrote, 'Whoever keeps His word, truly the love of God is perfected in Him. By this we know that we are in Him' (1 John 2:5). To keep My word is to do what I say. Obedience is the end result of love's full completeness. When you are hearing My voice and doing My will obediently from the heart, you know that My love is made complete in your life. Love is perfected and becomes complete as you seek My will and do it."

As Jesus spoke so passionately of this great love I was reminded of Paul's great summary of love in 1 Corinthians chapter 13. The chapter clearly defines and portrays love from the divine viewpoint. It personifies love and reminds us that love is not a thing but a person—God Himself.

Knowing my thoughts the Lord said assertively, "Paul's words in the love chapter remind us that love is the greatest gift one can possess. All the gifts of the spirit, knowledge, power, or religious devotion are worthless without love. Love never fails or comes to an end. It is eternal. The possessor of love possesses God in His fullness."

The Lord paused for a moment and then said tenderly, "My bride will walk in this fullness of love. She will prove the power of love. Her love for Me will demonstrate to the world that God is love. This love will not fail but will usher in the end of this age and the beginning of the age to come.

† Chapter 17: The Mystery of Suffering

As my meetings with the Lord take place I am in the midst of an enormous battle against disease. Even as I write these words I am fighting of a battle with Non-Hodgkins Lymphoma, a serious form of cancer. At one point I had lost over fifty pounds, my strength was completely drained, my heart rate was out of control and my appetite curtailed. The cancer had wrapped around the tube leading from my kidney to my bladder, creating a blockage in my kidney causing intense pain in my back.

During the early stages of this ordeal I lost all natural strength in my body. I was not able to do the simplest physical things. I was wasting away literally as I faced the greatest challenge of my life.

Then the Lord first appeared to me in the early morning of February 17 to begin His conversations with me at the seat of judgment. He has met me with tender love and grace each night since as we spend time together discussing my life journey on earth. In the midst of great suffering in my body the Lord came to me and began a work in my heart that is changing me forever.

As I consider all of this, the question of suffering has been at the front of my mind. I want to broach this question of suffering with the Lord but am hesitant for some reason. Perhaps this is because the question of suffering is always the first question that so many people want to ask Him. But, I know that I need the answer not only for myself but also for others who face suffering as followers of Christ.

"Lord," I blurted out, "I know there are unbelievers who mock you by saying, 'Why doesn't God just destroy the devil and all the evil he causes? If God is good by nature He would not allow suffering but would eliminate it because of His love.' They say this proves that you do not exist. Jesus, why is there such suffering in the world and how can it be reconciled with your great love?"

I have not seen anger in the Lord throughout our time together. This question, at the human level, would seem prime to illicit an angry response. I know that the question from others often made me angry.

There was no hint of such anger as the Lord divinely crafted His answer. In a compassionate tone He said, "I understand the concern people have about suffering. I suffered the pain of the cross. My body was a bloody mass of destruction when the brutality was over. And yet, the greatest pain was when My Father turned away from Me and the sin I bore for all mankind. My cry betrayed My pain, 'My God, My God why have you forsaken Me.'"

Jesus' eyes bubbled up. The tears slowly rolled down His face as He gravely measured the importance of the moment. In a whisper He began again: "I suffered and died for those who have mocked Me—for those who do not understand. I suffered death so that others could be freed from death's grip. I am saddened by the knowledge that many reject the provision I made for them."

Now, I was crying with the Lord. My tears exposed my realization that my sin was responsible for His suffering. Christ died for me personally. My sins put Him on the cross.

I cried with God. Together we sat quietly in tears. The moment was charged with intense feelings concerning the mystery of suffering. Now I was feeling awkward with my question. The question seemed so trivial at this point that I almost wished I hadn't asked it.

Jesus didn't wait for me to ask the question again. No doubt He sensed the need for me to have clarity on the matter of suffering.

He lovingly said, "I know that you are suffering even as we speak with the torment of this disease. You deserve to understand the mystery of suffering and how it is working in your life even now."

Timidly I responded to the Lord, "I know that you will explain why I'm suffering from cancer. From what is happening in my heart through our conversations, I feel I may already have that answer. But I am concerned for those who doubt you because they cannot understand suffering."

Jesus reached out to touch me at this point. His eyes glistened with teary compassion. At one point He closed His eyes as if readying Himself for His reply.

Then He replied, "Planet earth is at war. The war began when Lucifer rebelled against Me and brought the war to earth in the Garden of Eden. The enemy is out to destroy the human race and the promised seed of the first woman. He does not care about the people but only uses them for his own evil purpose.

"In war there is death and destruction, disease, and devastation in lives. The innocent along with the guilty are killed in war. War brings suffering to humanity."

I had not expected Jesus to explain the reason for suffering by talking about spiritual war. This beginning caught me by surprise. But as He shared I immediately realized the truth of His words. Suffering is the result of the great spiritual battle being fought against the forces of evil and their king, Satan, the god of this world system. My mind was now spinning with the implications of this war.

Jesus closed His eyes when He spoke of His enemy, as if troubled by having to place the adversary's name on His lips. He spoke of Satan with disdain but it was clear that He recognized the human implications of his evil.

In a serious tone He said, "Satan was a liar from the beginning. He is the enemy of the Great Shepherd and comes to steal, destroy and kill the sheep. His primary target is the Seed of the first woman, my brethren, my remnant bride, the church, because he knows that she is destined to bruise his head. He will stop at nothing in his maniacal plan to destroy those who embrace Me and My kingdom. Those who enter My family become his enemies and his targets."

As Jesus spoke my historical mind was reaching back over the epochs of history as I recalled the violent, death-filled history of planet earth. Wars, disease, dictators, murder, moral devastation, famine, persecution and much more run like a thread through earth's history.

The enemy had been quite successful in bringing evil to the world he dominated. And yet I realized as well that many Christians are oblivious to the origin of this evil and the reality of this great spiritual war.

"Lord," I began. "As you speak of spiritual war it becomes more real to me than I have ever realized. But many Christians of my time are not even aware that this war exists. They don't see the sin and evil as components of an organized strategy by a desperate but real spiritual enemy."

"Paul described the war so clearly: 'For we do not struggle against flesh and blood, but against spiritual rulers, against powers, against the rulers of the darkness of this age, against spiritual hordes of wickedness in the heavenly realm' (Eph. 6:12). Clearly the enemy has an organized army of demonic warriors in the spiritual realm. The Christian's battle is expressed often in the natural realm but the real battle is against Satan's demonic kingdom in the spiritual dimension."

Jesus took a deep breath and let it out as He readied His next words. His concern was evident. Then He spoke of the time of my life's journey.

He replied, "In the twentieth century My people forgot who they were. They saw themselves as a pep club for Me and they celebrated Me with much fanfare. They did not see that they were called to be a mighty spiritual army warring for the cause of My kingdom on earth.

"They played with the gifts of the Spirit as though they were toys instead of mighty instruments of warfare. I gave them supernatural weapons but they turned to human ingenuity for their strength and power. The war was being lost because My warriors were ignorant of the war and the enemy. But the rising up of the church would change all of that."

"Lord," I responded. "It seems that during that time the church took on a passive attitude about spiritual warfare. We avoided the spiritual war because it was dirty and real and we wanted everything orderly and peaceful."

"My early disciples realized immediately that they were in a war. Their Lord had been crucified before their eyes by the authorities of the day. My message was opposed by forces that could imprison them and even beat them and kill them. They stoned my servant Stephen to death for boldly proclaiming My word. Many others would suffer and die as they enlisted in My army to extend the realm of My kingdom."

Now there was a quiet fury in the Lord's words and on His face as He poured out His heart about His brave spiritual warriors of the first centuries.

He went on saying, "My last command to my disciples was 'All authority in heaven and earth has been given to Me. Go therefore and make disciples of all the nations, baptizing them in the name of the

Father and the Son and the Holy Spirit, teaching them to observe all that I have commanded you' (Matt. 28:18-20). I did not command them to merely get people saved but to make followers of them and to teach them to do the things I had commanded. They were enlisting warriors for My army who would go bravely into battle with the message of My kingdom."

At this point my mind was whirling with the reality of this spiritual war and the necessity of our commitment to it. I was sad that there had been times in my life when I too had shirked my responsibility as a warrior in God's army.

The Lord picked up where He left off saying firmly, "Paul understood the nature of this battle. He cried out, '...that I may know Him and the power of His resurrection, and the fellowship of His sufferings, being conformed to His death.' The apostle knew that to enter the battle one must share in My sufferings, being willing to face the attack of the enemy in obedience to Me. The body of Christ is called to continue My ministry upon the earth, extending My kingdom through the proclamation of My word."

As the Lord spoke, I was thinking of Paul's statement, "I now rejoice in my sufferings for you, and fill in my flesh what is lacking in the afflictions of Christ, for the sake of His body, the church" (Col. 1:24). Paul rejoiced in His sufferings because he knew they were necessary for the sake of the church. He realized that Christ's afflictions continued because He was in His body and His body continued to be attacked by the enemy.

Suffering is the direct result of demonic reaction to the extension of My rule. The enemy will attack and counter attack but the church must know what Paul knew when he said, "He who is in you is greater than he who is in the world" (1 John 4: 4).

We serve a Lord vastly greater than the god of this world. His kingdom is established on love, the greatest power in the universe. He is the Creator while Satan is a created, fallen being. Satan's power comes through deception and propaganda. The power of God is the good news of the salvation Christ secured on the cross. This message liberates people from their sin and religious works and transforms people into kingdom warriors.

Jesus took persecution against His church as persecution against Himself. He had declared to Saul on the road to Damascus, "Saul, Saul, why are you persecuting Me?...I am Jesus whom you are persecuting" (Acts 9: 4, 5). With such verses swirling in my mind I was becoming very aware that suffering and spiritual warfare were an integral part of God's plan.

But I also knew that I had lived much of my Christian experience in an environment in which Christians seemed to want to avoid conflict and suffering. They had even developed doctrines to avoid the reality of suffering and spiritual warfare. Most Christians, rather than having to face the persecution of the end times, expected a dramatic rapture rescue to save them from suffering. We did not understand suffering because we avoided the battle to which the Lord calls us.

Having been a historian most of my life, I was intrigued by the Lord's next statements. He used World War II to exemplify the nature of spiritual war: "In your second great war," He began, "Hitler and his military had extended his power over all of Europe. His authority and power had replaced all influence on the continent. He was entrenched in the continent and would not move from his position unless some invading force came against him. The Allied nations knew this to be true. They would have to invade the coast of Europe and begin a struggle to regain the captured territory.

"The allies knew instinctively that many would die and be injured in this attempt. The enemy cannot be routed without casualties. As the beaches of Normandy were taken many brave soldiers died and suffered but they moved ever forward toward the completion of their mission. They captured the coasts and then began their march across Europe liberating the continent one portion at a time. Many died and suffered the ravages of war but the evil empire was defeated and freedom restored."

After a pause the Lord continued saying, "Satan has extended his power in the same way. He has taken control of large areas of planet earth. My church, My spiritual army, is commissioned to storm the gates of Hell. Did I not say, 'I will build My church and the gates of Hell shall not prevail against it' (Matt. 16: 18).

"Just as the Allies invaded and liberated Europe, I have called My church to invade and liberate the territory of Satan. His hellish kingdom cannot stand against the weapons of warfare I provide. Remember, 'All authority has been given to Me.' The victory has already been won through the cross and the glory it released."

I spoke out at this time a monumental understatement: "So, Lord, if we are taking the fight to the enemy we must expect suffering along the way. If we are to penetrate Satan's kingdom with your word we must expect fierce opposition."

Jesus let out a deep, long sigh as He took in a breath and let it out slowly. He was obviously going to say something that touched His heart deeply. I sensed sadness and great pride in His voice as He began.

Sadly He said, "My entire inner circle of disciples except John suffered as martyrs. Some were crucified, beheaded, beaten to death, thrust through with sword or spear or stoned to death. My followers were imprisoned, burned at the stake, fed to animals, and cruelly mistreated in many ways. They were willing to suffer and die for Me because I was real in their lives and the message they carried was setting people free."

I added, "And they understood that they were part of a vast army of spiritual warriors who believed enough in their cause to suffer and die if need be!"

The Lord, continuing His point, replied, "True. They believed and their faith produced courageous works in their lives."

He paused, now, as if wanting to say something else. He turned his head to look directly into my eyes and began, "And now about you My son."

Immediately I began to cry for I knew what the Lord meant. He had cleared up the matter of suffering but now I sensed He would address my personal situation with cancer.

"I know the weakness you are experiencing. The disease has taken its toll on your natural strength. This season of testing is for your blessing and for My glory. My grace is sufficient for you. My strength in you is being perfected in you through this weakness.

"Whereas unbelievers are often healed in your midst because they need a sign, I discipline My children. I turn the attacks of the enemy into opportunities for My children. Paul had to leave Trophimus in Miletus because he was sick. I used this time alone with my sick disciple to bless his life in special ways.

"I am blessing you in special ways as well. I am causing the church to rise up around you as a visible confirmation of the message you bear. It is not enough that you have My message. You must be that message in the core of your being. When this season of testing is complete there will be a new beginning for you and the body of Christ."

I was humbled by His words. I had already perceived much of what the Lord said, but hearing Him say it was a special blessing. My theme verse during this ordeal has been from Isaiah, "They that wait upon the Lord shall renew their strength. They shall mount up with wings like eagles. They shall run and not be weary. They shall walk and not faint" (Isa. 40:31).

I am waiting on Him and my strength is being renewed.

† Chapter 18: Forgiveness

Satan's war is fueled by the power of sin. Through these times with the Lord I have come to a simple definition of sin. It is acting apart from the will of God. Often we think of sin as this long list of evil deeds that displease God. We wrongly think that if we can just stay off of that list of deeds that we are living a life free of sin. Sin was introduced in the Garden when the first humans acted independently of God. They simply chose to do what they wanted instead of what God had said.

I am often brought back in my thinking on this subject to a passage in James:

> Come now, you who say, "Today or tomorrow we will go to such and such a city, spend a year there, buy and sell, and make a profit." But you do not know what tomorrow will bring. For what is your life? It is even a vapor that appears for a little time and then vanishes away. Instead you should say, "If the Lord wills, we shall live and do this or that." But now you boast in your self sufficiency. All such boasting is evil (James 4:13-16).

The passage shows that to merely say you are going to make certain plans for the future without considering the Lord's will and then boast about it is evil. The word for "evil" here is a very strong word indicating wickedness at the highest level. To make certain plans for the future may not in itself be an evil action, but to do so without consulting the Lord is serious sin.

Jesus wants us to yoke with Him in that we abandon our individual lives and walk along with Him. He promises to bear the burden if we will simply allow ourselves to be yoked with Him. But this means allowing Him control of our lives. It means submitting to His will in matters of life. This is the life of the bondservant, one who has voluntarily given Himself to the Lord for His will and purpose.

Knowing the seriousness of sin brings to mind the importance of forgiveness in the lives of followers of Christ. It is inevitable that we and people in our lives will stumble occasionally, bringing up the need for forgiveness and its healing power.

Seeing the forgiving nature in Jesus, I wanted to see this divine quality through His eyes. I ventured forth asking, "Lord, I know that you make some serious comments about forgiveness in your word. Obviously, you consider it more seriously than we Christians."

Jesus, shaking His head in agreement, answered, "Forgiveness is treating others and yourself through the finished work of the cross. When people walk in lack of forgiveness toward others or even themselves, they mock the cross and what it stands for. When I was teaching My disciples to pray I gave them a warning saying, 'For if you forgive men their sins, your heavenly Father will forgive you. But if you do not forgive men their sins, neither will your Father forgive your sins'" (Matt. 6:14, 15).

"I have read that passage many times and am troubled by what it seems to be saying," I replied. "Your words seem to imply that God holds us accountable for our sins when we hold others accountable for theirs. Lord, it seems to me that if you are holding me accountable for my sins that I would therefore suffer the eternal penalty for sin."

Sternly the Lord continued. "Forgiveness is the truest mark of the converted heart. The forgiven person knows how to forgive. The person who lacks forgiveness toward another is assuming the position of God—a grave error. Such a person is mocking the cross from which I said, 'Father, forgive them for they do not know what they do.'

"It is a serious matter to walk in a state of unforgiveness. It alienates a person from Me and My forgiveness. I commanded My disciples, 'Do not judge, and you will not be judged. Do not condemn, and you will not be condemned. Forgive, and you will be forgiven' (Luke 6:36). In this matter of judgment and forgiveness you will reap in your life what you sew. Learn to sew forgiveness and leave the judgment to Me."

I replied, "Lord, there was a time in my life when I could not forgive myself for things I had done. The glaring nature of my sin was so strong that I could not imagine you could forgive me, so I certainly couldn't forgive myself."

Jesus replied by quoting from Paul's writings. "'There is therefore no condemnation to those who are in Christ Jesus. For the law of the Spirit of life has set you free in Christ Jesus from the law of sin and death' (Rom. 8: 1, 2). In Me there is no condemnation, so the crucial thing is to be in Me."

"Aren't all Christians in you Lord?" I asked.

Jesus answered quickly, "No. Those who allow themselves to be led by the flesh step out of Me and go their own way. They become open to condemnation by sin through the Accuser of the brethren. They are born again but choose to live by the flesh which leads to death or separation from Me and My life. Condemnation will mark their lives. In this same passage Paul says, 'Those who are led by the Spirit are the sons of God.' (8:14). Those who allow My Spirit to dwell in them and lead them will know the freedom of sonship in Me."

"You mentioned the Accuser of the brethren," I responded. "Certainly he wants God's people to walk in the flesh and experience condemnation."

"He wants to enslave people to sin and then use it to condemn their hearts," Jesus replied. "I am your Advocate. I am the Mediator between God and man. I argue your cause before the throne of heaven. Satan is the prosecuting attorney. He wants to find you guilty so he can pronounce your guilty judgment. He is the Accuser of the brethren."

Of course the church is ever on my mind so I wanted to know how the wineskin of the body of Christ applied to this situation. "Lord, if we are in you, will we not also be in your body, the church?"

"The church is the community of the forgiven. The healthy gathering of the saints dispels sin, condemnation, and unforgiveness from its members. The four elements of church life—the word, fellowship, breaking of bread, and prayers—consistently protect the saints from sin and condemnation. The word brings My truth to bear. By fellowship the word is distributed into the lives of the brethren. The communion meal is always present, reminding the saints of My shed blood and broken body. Through prayer the saints commune with Me and allow My Spirit to lead them into truth. Yes, to be in Me is to be in My body. Those who try to live the Spirit-led life apart from life in My church will fall short."

I responded, "It seems like it always comes down to our commitment to life in the body of Christ. I see why Satan works so hard to keep us from continuous union with God's people. He wants to isolate us so he can rob us of spiritual strength and then devour us."

"You touch on a crucial truth," Jesus added. "The greatest deception of the enemy is that the Christian life can be lived in isolation—that it is simply an individual experience. It has an individual beginning but a corporate expression. The baby Christian is born into a family, the church. The church is not just a doctrine but a context in which My followers can truly be nourished and grow in Me."

"The community of the forgiven," I replied. "I love that expression, Lord. The church is a special haven in which forgiveness can flourish. We have missed this important truth and so many are not able to forgive themselves and others. They miss the reality of the cross."

"Missing this community of the forgiven," He continued, "My people tend to rate their sins. They think that some sins are worse than others. Many fall for the lie that their personal sins are so awful that My forgiveness cannot reach them. Such thinking belittles the power of the cross and My shed blood. If you confess your sins, I am faithful and just to forgive them and cleanse you from all unrighteousness. I died to make it so."

Now tears began to bubble up in my eyes. His words had struck a chord deep in my soul. I now saw that I had wasted so much time in my life because I did not understand the completeness of His work on the cross. My eyes caught His and together we looked down at the blood on the mercy seat. Neither of us had to say a word.

† Chapter 19: Entering God's Rest

As I write these words I am troubled that some of my cancer symptoms have worsened. My heart rate is back up. My energy level is down again and I have a fever in the evenings again.

These symptoms had gone away at one point and my hope was that they would not return. Though I am meeting with the Lord in the night time hours, my daily life is still filled with the details of the struggle against this disease.

The cancer treatment caused a blood clot in my left leg. This requires taking blood thinning medication. At first this was taken by means of a self-administered shot in the stomach followed by pills to regulate the thickening of blood. At one point the blood thinners caused a serious hemorrhage of the blood vessels in my left eye. My eye literally filled up with blood one night when the blood vessels broke.

Recently my red blood cells were so low that I developed serious anemia which causes brutal fatigue. This requires taking a shot in the stomach once a week for four weeks to restore the blood cells. All of these things have resulted in multiple trips to the doctors for blood tests, appointments and treatment. Most weeks we are traveling to Fresno, forty-five minutes away, two and three times a week.

I say all of this not to draw attention to my sickness but to show the context in which I am seeking to enter and remain in God's rest. My theme verse throughout this ordeal has been from Isaiah, "They that wait upon the Lord shall renew their strength; they shall mount up with wings like eagles, They shall run and not be weary. They shall walk and not faint" (Isa. 40:31). Learning to genuinely wait upon the Lord—to rest in Him—may be the most difficult lesson of my life.

My friend and brother in the Lord, Dan, came by yesterday to encourage us. He shared with us verses from Psalm 37. The passage speaks of three actions that we must take to enter the rest of God: trust in the Lord, delight in the Lord, and commit our way to the Lord. Then the Psalmist says, "Rest in the Lord, and wait patiently for Him" (v. 7). If I am trusting that God will do what He promises, delighting myself in His presence, and committing my way to Him, I should be able to find rest in Him.

When one has cancer, trusting God means believing that God is in control and that His will is being done. Fear of the disease must bow to the knowledge that God has promised victory over it. This trust leads to delight in the Lord because His presence becomes so real. In this atmosphere we gain the desire to commit our way to Him.

Ken, a precious brother in the Lord, came forward at a gathering of the saints in Monterey, California. As he laid hands on me to pray he declared from the Lord, "You will be healed and you will have the victory. Your work has only just begun and I have much for you to do."

His prophetic prayer lifted my heart and gave me a wonderful sense of victory that carried over to this moment. God's promise helped me stay in His rest.

If my way is given to God I have nothing left to do but rest in Him and wait on Him because My pathway no longer belongs to me but is in His hands. Rest comes from knowing that what the Psalmist calls "my way," the course of my life, is not up to me but up to Him.

But this is all doctrine and theory unless it is working in our lives. Resting in God is the end result of knowing Him fully. I want to know Him fully and rest in His presence even when I am in the middle of a great struggle.

I knew that Jesus understood. He sees our needs long before we express them to Him. He knows our hearts better than we do. Here in the most restful place in the universe, I asked Him about rest.

"Lord," I said, "the struggle I face now sometimes pulls me away from the rest I have in you. The changing symptoms of this disease often cause me to take my eyes off of you and set them on the circumstances. When this happens I lose your peace and sense disorder in my spirit. I need to know how to maintain my rest in you."

"Let Me tell you a true story that will help," the Lord replied. "The multitude was surrounding us so I said to the disciples, 'Let us cross over to the other side.' Ministering to the multitude had made Me tired so I went to sleep on a pillow in the stern of the boat as we made our way to the far side. A violent storm arose as I was sleeping and caused the waves to beat against the boat. My disciples became fearful and awakened Me with the rebuke, 'Teacher, do you not care that we are perishing?' I'm sure you know how I reacted. I rebuked the storm and it became calm.

"I said to them, 'Why are you so fearful? How is it that you do not have faith?'"

"I've read that story many times," I said. "I think I would have reacted exactly the way the disciples did. The storm was very real so they became fearful. They knew you would do something if you knew about the storm so they woke you up."

Jesus smiled that smile that said, I understand what you're saying but you have missed the point. With a confirming smile He responded, "You have missed the main point of this event. Let me ask you a question that might help. Why do you suppose they became so fearful?"

"It seems like a normal thing for people to be afraid of a violent storm, especially when they think it is threatening their safety," I answered.

Responding to my concern He said, "I taught my disciples to rise above what is normal—to live in communion with Me and rise to life in the Spirit. No, they were afraid because they were not resting in Me. Remember that I said to them, 'Let us cross over to the other side.' When My word is clear you can rest on it. What I say reveals what is really true beyond the circumstances of life.

"If they had heard what I said and trusted Me, they would have been at rest as the storm arose. In that rest, fear could not have arisen in their hearts. Had they not been fearful their faith would have risen up and they would have been able to rebuke the storm and let Me continue My restful sleep."

"I never saw it that way before," I replied. "But as you explain it I now see that they were not really resting in you or the fear would not have arisen."

"Yes," He went on, "fear is the enemy of faith. Fear turns your eyes from God and sets them on the physical circumstances and produces works of the flesh. Fear convinced them that they were perishing while I was a few feet away. Fear ignored the fact that I had spoken and was with them. Faith turns you to God's way of thinking on the matter and sets your eyes on what He is doing and what He has said. Faith performs signs and wonders because it is the spiritual power that implements what God has spoken."

"But, Lord, I still don't understand why you expected them to be in a place of rest even before the storm arose. How would rest have developed in their lives?" I questioned.

Jesus tilted His head to the side and gave me a look of loving concern as He answered saying, "They were with Me and I was at rest. I had said to them earlier, 'Come to Me all who labor and are heavy laden and I will give you rest. Take My yoke upon you and learn from Me, for I am humble and lowly in heart, and you will find rest for your souls.' Rest is the result of being in My presence. To yoke with Me is to walk with Me and receive the rest in which I live."

"But Lord, they had been with you for some time. Why had they not learned to receive your rest? Surely your presence was enough."

"My presence is always enough," He went on. "But I said something else in the verse—'and learn from Me.' My followers are those who go where I go and learn from Me. Learning from me is a simple matter of listening to what I say and observing My example. They were in My school of discipleship and still had some lessons to learn."

As I revisit this conversation I have just returned home after a week in isolation in the hospital as the doctors tried to discover the source of a fever I had developed. Since my white blood cells were dangerously low, I was susceptible to infection from any bacteria or virus that came along.

After a week of blood tests, two chest X-rays, a CT scan, a biopsy of fluid in my lung, an EKG, heart scan, and numerous other examinations, the doctors still could not say definitively what caused my fever. I got to know some wonderful nurses and staff members but the tedium of hospital life was wearing on me. It is good to be home again.

With all of this in mind I returned to my question asking, "Lord, I feel like I have so much to learn on this matter of resting. There are times when I feel like I am being distracted by the circumstances. Hospital life seemed especially designed to pull me from my rest in you."

In the back of my mind the question, "Why did I have to go through all of that?" kept swirling around. I didn't verbalize this concern because I felt the Lord had previously dealt with it.

But the Lord cares more about what is in our hearts than the words on our lips. His response addressed what was in my heart. "Why do you always evaluate the importance of an experience solely on the basis of how it affected you?"

"But Lord, how else can I evaluate a stay in the hospital?" I quickly responded.

His response was equally quick, "By how it affected others! What about the people in the hospital I sent you to bless?"

I was momentarily surprised by what Jesus had just said. But my mind quickly flashed back to my hospital stay. The redeeming aspect of the stay was the many encounters I had with the nurses and other staff members. God's anointing concerning His rest had been on my heart entering the hospital and carried over into wonderful conversations and encounters with those who served me.

They treated me like royalty and I shared with them the restful, blessed, spirit my King had given me. Now I realized that I was not in the hospital just for medical help but to bless and be blessed by the people. God's perspective is always so much bigger than mine.

The Lord continued, "If you have truly entered My rest you will look for My purpose in every circumstance. You will realize that I am causing everything to work together for good. You will not always ask 'How is it affecting me?' but will understand that I am touching other lives as well. I am quite capable of doing many things at once, touching many lives in the process."

"I see what you mean, Lord. In order to truly rest I have to get past my self and enter into what you are doing," I responded.

"Yes," He agreed, "My word says, 'For whoever has entered God's rest has also rested from his works as God did from His' (Heb. 4:10). In order to enter My rest you must rest from your own works, the activities that elevate self instead of God. You cannot rest in Me when your own works dominate your life."

"How does this all apply to the Sabbath Day commandment of the Old Testament?" I asked.

"I came to earth to fulfill the law," the Lord began. "The law was completed in Me. I became the law. Through the Holy Spirit I have come to dwell in you. By the Spirit, the law is within you—it is written on your hearts. Before I came, the law was written on stone and was a mere external guide for my people. The Sabbath day reminded them to rest from their worldly works and to come apart to Me."

I was beginning to see what the Lord was saying but I knew that some Christians believe that the Sabbath is still in effect. I knew that the Sabbath was not mentioned in the New Testament beyond the Gospels and was not a practice of the early church.

Jesus continued saying, "The Sabbath was fulfilled in Me. As you enter My rest in your daily life you fulfill the Sabbath. It is not about a certain day of the week but a daily walk with Me by the Spirit. Christianity was never meant to be a set of rules, regulations, and ritual but a way of life in which My people are led by the Spirit daily."

I am amazed, as these conversations with Jesus continue, how much depends on simply being led by the Spirit. As we allow the Spirit to lead us daily so many questions and concerns fade away in the glorious radiance of His presence. To be with Jesus and to be led by Him is the answer to every question.

† Chapter 20: Finances in the Kingdom

I am realizing that God approaches things that involve His people in a very simple fashion. Unlike religious people, God is not trying to be sophisticated and complicated with us. He tells it like it is in very common understandable language. During His earthly ministry He communicated with stories, parables, and simple, clear language.

Christians and the organized church have drastically complicated the issue of finances in the church. I have very strong feelings about this issue but I wanted to hear God's perspective.

"Lord," I ventured out, "It seems to me that one of the most complicated issues in the organized church today is the matter of finances. I was wondering how you view this matter."

The Lord closed His eyes, pursed His lips and shook His head slowly back and forth. I had obviously broached an area about which the Lord had strong feelings.

"In the beginning," He began, "My church was very simple by design. It was people gathering in My honor to build one another up. They gathered where it was convenient, in homes, alongside rivers, in parks and other settings.

"The church is made up of those who hear My call, come out of the world and gather to Me. It is My church and I will build it according to My will. No man can build My church. When men build something they build it according to their own will and purpose and at that point it ceases to be the church."

"Your vision of the church is so simple," I added. "But men have tried to organize the church so that it fits a certain pattern that they like. Is this why there is so much abuse in the area of money?"

"I pay My own way," the Lord began. "If I have purposed something, I will provide the finances for it. But when men move outside of My purpose they must provide their own means of financing. They must find a way to pay for buildings, salaries, and special programs they have initiated.

"They must move outside of the realm of the Spirit into the world of flesh to provide for the organized program they have instigated. The outcome is something of man, something of the flesh, not the simple manifestation of My church."

"It looks to me like the way we use money corresponds to our vision of your church," I volunteered. "It seems to me that if people have your simple view of the church they will have a simple view of finances."

"Exactly," Jesus agreed. "The New Testament speaks of only two uses of money by My church. First, the truly needy within the church should be cared for. Secondly, elders and workers beyond the local church who labor in My kingdom should be considered worthy of financial help.

"These are to be gifts based on need and the leading of My Spirit not ongoing salaries. No person should be allowed to be a hireling of the church. My people should give consistently into the local church in which they are fed and into apostolic ministries as I lead."

"The organized church has long since rejected that simplicity." I responded. "They have developed many other things to spend money on."

He quickly responded, "When controlling men took over the church they were on their own in regard to finances. Without My support they turned to effective business methods for raising money, and running a business. They purchased buildings, paid salaries and developed programs that fit their agenda. They did all of this without My assistance or support.

"Using the business methods of the world, they set out to do whatever they set their minds to. The problem is they did not build My church but a well-financed religious business. My presence was not in it because they had not consulted Me or invited Me to participate."

It was heart-rending to hear the Lord explain how the organized church had developed and how it used the business methods of the world. It was sad to see that men could simply proceed without consulting with God because they had become so confident in their own natural ability. When they abandoned the simplicity of the church they had to develop worldly financing methods to pay for their complicated institutions.

"Lord, I know that many organized churches emphasize tithing as a means of raising money for their programs," I commented. "How does tithing fit into your plan for the church?"

"Giving in the church was to be by the leading of the Holy Spirit. Tithing was an external, fleshly standard of giving established as the inheritance of the Levites, the priestly tribe of Israel. The tithe paid for their livelihood and for the activities of the temple. In the New Testament, the church is the temple and there is no priestly class. Every believer is a priest unto Me and I am the High Priest of this new spiritual priesthood."

Jesus was adamant on this subject. He is serious about everything that affects His church. His sharing on this matter of tithing brought to my mind how many organized churches tend to bring elements of the Old Testament into their practice when it is convenient for their program.

I asked Him about this tendency. "Lord, many organized churches seem to bring Old Testament principles and practices into the New Testament church."

With an agreeing nod of His head Jesus answered declaring, "The New Covenant is based on My blood and the leadership of the Holy Spirit. This covenant was not based on a physical temple, a priestly class, or a temple monetary system. The covenant I made in My blood established a church in which My people are all priests unto Me.

"Every believer may come directly to My throne without any human mediator. The temple is made up of My people who are the stones with which I am building a spiritual house to My glory. Giving in My temple—the church—is under the guidance of My Holy Spirit. Every believer is to give as He is led by My Spirit. Every activity of the church is to be by the inner leading of My Spirit, not by an external decree or regulation."

Jesus paused for a moment as if readying Himself to make a significant point. He tilted His head toward me with a serious expression and continued, "I did not die to create another religion. I died, was buried, resurrected and glorified, so that I could send the Holy Spirit to My church. The Holy Spirit came into your lives to lead you and guide you into all truth. He would disclose to you everything pertaining to the will of My Father. Life in My church is to be a life led by the Spirit. The sons of God are those who are led by the Spirit of God.

"Many have turned My church into a religion with a priestly class of leaders, a physical temple in which they worship, and a monetary system borrowed from the Old Testament. They have moved from being led by My Spirit to being led by human traditions and religious practices."

The Lord's serious demeanor moved me to respond, "Lord I have seen that your church is so very simple and everything connected to it is simple. You have not created a complicated religion but a simple way of family life and you have communicated it to us in clear fashion in your word."

Agreeing, the Lord replied, "Giving in My church is part of that simplicity. Paul wrote, 'So let each one give as he purposes in his heart, not grudgingly or under compulsion, for God loves a cheerful giver.' This is the New Testament principle of giving. My people are to seek God's will in giving, purpose in their heart to give accordingly and then give with a cheerful heart of generosity.

"The church in its simplest form has few needs. A simple fund established to care for the needy is sufficient. Saints are to give into that fund as the Spirit leads and the funds are to be used as He leads. This simple way was the practice of My early church until men complicated things with religion."

I broke in, "You made that important point with the incident involving Ananias and Sapphira."

"What a sad affair that was," the Lord responded. "They had sold some property and then purposed in their hearts to hold some of the proceeds back while making it appear that they were giving it all. They were lying to the Holy Spirit. They were not being compelled by anyone to give a certain amount.

"They could have purposed to keep everything if that was what they wanted. Instead they decided to purpose one thing and do another.

Their untimely deaths drew attention to the importance of giving from the heart as the Holy Spirit moves."

I could not help but say, "Your saints were being moved to sell possessions and lay them at the feet of the apostles who were distributing to the needs of the saints. There were no needy among them because everyone was sharing what they had."

The Lord continued my thought. "It was the principle of the body working in regard to finances. By the Holy Spirit they knew that they were members of one another and that what they owned belonged to all members of the body of Christ. When My people realize that they are members of My body they do not hold onto their possessions in a selfish way but realize that all they possess belongs to Me and to the church.

"When I said, 'Present your bodies a living sacrifice,' I was imploring you to give yourselves to Me and to your brothers and sisters. You are members of one another in My Spirit."

"But some, Lord, teach a doctrine of prosperity," I added. "They teach that it is your will that every believer prosper financially. They teach that as believers are faithful to tithe into a ministry they will receive a hundred-fold return and thus experience financial prosperity."

"My promise is that if you seek first the kingdom of God and His righteousness that all of your physical needs will be met. I said, 'And God is able to make all grace abound to you, so that having all sufficiency in all things at all times, you may have an abundance for every good work' (2 Cor. 9:8).

"This passage was not written concerning giving into some ministry but giving toward the needs of the saints. As My people give from a cheerful heart I make sure that they continue to have their needs met and that they have an abundance for continued good works. This truth is not to make you rich but to assure that the needs of My body are met."

After a purposed pause, the Lord gave me a stern look and continued, "Some have turned their ministry into a means of financial gain. Paul worked with his hands making tents to assure that the churches were not burdened. Some gave into his ministry but he never put pressure on them to do so. Giving is to be voluntary, from the heart, not coerced with a promise of riches. The purpose of all giving is to meet the needs of My people, the church."

It seems that every conversation we have together leads to this simple understanding of the church. So many doctrines of Scripture are misunderstood because we do not see the simplicity of the church as revealed in the word. Every doctrine is best understood in the light of knowing and loving God through Christ and loving His people.

The church is the expression of that love. The simple truths of God's word are easily understood in the light of His clear, simple will for His church. God give us the grace to see and understand.

† Chapter 21: Worship

In 1963, the year I came to Christ, a typical church service involved singing a hymn or two, a special musical number, perhaps a choir presentation, announcements, an offering, the sermon, and an altar call. There was little spontaneity and everything of course was done just as it was recorded in the morning bulletin.

Today the hymns and the musical number have been replaced by what is commonly referred to as "the worship service." A worship band leads the congregation in a series of worship and praise songs while the song lyrics are projected onto a screen overhead. The worship service is followed by announcements, an offering, the obligatory sermon by the pastor and perhaps an altar call.

All of this is, of course, clearly spelled out in the morning bulletin. Most evangelical Christians think of the musical part of the program as the time of worship. The highlight of the service is the eloquent sermon delivered by the pastor.

I remember when this transition to a worship service took place. The charismatic revival was underway and many churches were tired of the old hymnal and its traditional songs. At first some churches would sing a few choruses without the use of a song book or hymnal.

Participants gradually became more active by clapping their hands to the rhythm or raising their hands to the Lord.

The spontaneous participation of the believers was seen as a real breakthrough. At first the music was quite simple with a piano or keyboard and perhaps a guitar. Eventually, full blown bands became the norm. It is a rare church today that does not have a least a couple of guitars, a keyboard, drums, and a worship leader.

I wondered what the Lord thought of the way many churches worship Him. I was quite surprised by His quick and straightforward response to my question.

"I am blessed" He began, "when My children worship Me from the heart. I am delighted when I see My people abandon themselves to Me in songs of praise and worship. These are moments of great joy for Me. I draw near when My people express love to Me from their hearts. I inhabit the praises of the saints."

The Lord hesitated in the middle of His response. He seemed to be pondering something else that softened His enthusiasm. His head lifted to the heavenly horizon and eyes seemed to search for His next words.

Quietly He said, "Whether someone is singing a song, praising, praying, or just having a sit-down conversation with Me, it is the heart that matters. I do not look on the exterior of man but always look at the heart. I care not for certain music styles or for how beautiful one can sing. The style and loudness of the music do not concern Me. I am concerned with the condition of the heart."

His eyes remained fixed on the horizon as He spoke. He was commenting on something very dear to His heart and His searching eyes betrayed His feelings. I somehow knew what He was going to say before He said it.

"To obey is better than sacrifice," the words came slowly. "I would rather hear a man who sings out of tune from his heart than the greatest choir the world has to offer. When a saint is doing something from the heart it will be followed with obedience. Without obedience to the truth of the words being sung, there is no true worship. Empty motions that produce no real change in one's life are simply religion. Religion goes through the motions of sacrifice without obedience."

As I pondered what the Lord was saying I thought of those many times when I sang the songs of a worship service. The words called us to obedience. Some of the songs were so powerful that if a church just obeyed the words of one song, repentance and revival would break out in their midst.

The problem is that the singing often becomes a rote, mindless, repetition of words without the desire to obey what they say. When the heart is disconnected from the singing there is no true worship and the lives of the people remain unchanged.

The Lord continued His thought: "I have said, 'Why do you call Me Lord, Lord, and not do the things which I say.' Often in their singing My saints are crying out 'Lord, Lord' but there is little obedience to the words they sing. King David in his repentance said, 'The sacrifices of God are a broken spirit, a broken and contrite heart' (Ps. 51:7). David's heart was broken when he realized his sin. He repented because his heart was broken and cut off from fellowship with Me. Such a broken heart leads to obedience. Without obedience worship is not complete. Faith without works is dead."

"Lord," I broke in. "It seems that every subject we talk about comes back somehow to the simplicity of your church. In leaving that simplicity of fellowship around you we have developed an entertainment-oriented church gathering. Instead of coming to participate, many come expecting a musical concert."

"There are times when the church should come together to celebrate through joyous singing and praise to Me. Let the instruments make their joyful noise and let the people rejoice in My presence. Let them dance before Me free from the restraints of religion. Let some who are gifted in singing lift their voices in singular praise to Me. Let spontaneous songs spring up from the saints as they are guided and inspired by My Holy Spirit."

Jesus was smiling as He described this joyous celebration of the church. It was not hard to see that He enjoyed music and the Spirit-led use of music and singing. His face was lit up with an expression of heavenly joy as He talked about the church gathered to celebrate Him. But then the big smile became a pondering frown as His eyes again searched the horizon.

Continuing, He said, "Celebrating in a large group with such joyous celebration serves a good purpose in My kingdom. But the ongoing gatherings of My church are to be family meetings. They are to be the intimate gatherings of smaller groups where each person can participate as the Spirit leads. My word must be lifted up and be prayerfully considered in the context of open sharing.

"As truth is spoken in love and applied to their lives the saints are built up and the church grows. By the Spirit I can facilitate the gathering of every group and guide the spiritual flow of the meeting. Prayers, lessons, testimonies, songs, gifts of the Spirit and other ways of sharing should take place. The diversity of My people will be expressed and such participation will produce true spiritual growth and bring real unity and the release of My power."

As Jesus said these words I was reminded again at how often the concerns I have come back to Jesus' simple understanding of His church. This question of worship has its answer in understanding how He wants us to gather and how we are to conduct ourselves when we are together.

The concert-oriented gathering with loud music and full band is not conducive to intimate meetings where all can participate and Christ is the guest of honor guiding the meeting by the Spirit. It is entertainment oriented and discourages active participation.

On the other hand these smaller groups can occasionally gather in large groups in a larger building for a celebration that involves music and singing and joyous expressions of love to God and His people. Such large celebrations would encourage unity and relationship between smaller home groups and protect against the tendency to become isolated. The early church, for example, met from house to house but also gathered in the temple in large groups (Acts 2:46).

I was excited about Jesus' enthusiasm for music and genuine worship from the heart. On the other hand, I could also see that He is saddened when our forms of worship become rote and religious. He does not care about the outward form but is keenly interested in the condition of our hearts.

During one of my many hospital visits Mary and I experienced this first hand. We had rushed to the doctor when my bladder would not empty itself. Because of a stint they had inserted from my kidney to my bladder, blood clots were dropping down into my bladder and eventually blocked up my ability to eliminate. We were in the emergency room for eight hours in this condition as we waited for a specialist to come.

This was on Easter morning and just happened to be our wedding anniversary. What a way to celebrate an anniversary— spending time in the hospital emergency room with a blocked bladder. At one point my precious wife began to sing the song *He is Lord*.

I joined in and in the midst of our turmoil we worshipped our Lord and declared that He has risen from the dead and is indeed Lord. We sang several songs that evening as we paused to remember the gift of life He had given us. We had experienced worship in its highest form, for Jesus was there with us joining us in song as we praised Him and gave Him the glory He is due. What a joy it is to worship our God!

† Chapter 22: Mary

I am blessed to have Mary as my wife. She is to me the earthly representation of the bride of Christ. I see in her the glory of my God and am reminded daily by her beauty that Jesus will one day have His beautiful bride.

I have an expression that I learned from one of my favorite movies, *Quigley Down Under*. In the movie the main character, played by Tom Selleck, says to the leading lady, "You sure look pretty in the morning sun."

I changed the words to, "You sure look pretty in the morning light," and regularly look for opportunities to say them to my beautiful wife. Her beauty goes beyond her natural physical beauty into the spiritual beauty of Christ within her.

While I was on one of my hospital stays during my cancer treatment, I would wait at the hospital window on the third floor to wave at her as she was leaving or coming. My heart leaped like the heart of a teenager when she waved back. I love her more than words can describe.

I first set my eyes on Mary in world history class at Shafter High School in California. When I saw her come through the classroom door I immediately knew that pretty lady was someone I would like to know better. Little did I know that she was the woman that God had picked out to be my wife.

One day I finally got up the nerve to ask her out on a date. The problem was that I was not a believer but Mary had been raised in a Christian home. She struggled with this for some time but finally consented to go with me to the local drive-in theater, the entertainment of choice in those days. I was a bit shy so we eased into our relationship gradually.

It was the third date before Mary introduced me to our first kiss. That was a moment I will never forget. She stood on the small porch at the front door of their house and our lips met for the first time. I have been deeply in love with her since those early days.

We've had our normal ups and downs but my love for her has deepened in ways that are hard to describe. Through my love for her I can better understand the love Jesus has for His bride. I can understand how He was willing to die for her. His love drove Him to the ultimate sacrifice. Our marriage has produced two of the most wonderful children, Matthew and Karis. They have truly blessed us in so many ways and are a reflection of the love Mary and I have for one another.

That is why Christ commands husbands "To love your wives as Christ also loved the church and gave Himself for her, that He might sanctify and cleanse her with the washing of water in the word, that He might present to Himself a glorious church, not having spot or wrinkle or any such things, but that she should be holy and without blemish" (Eph. 5: 25-27).

Many Christian men miss the point that this is a command from God through His apostle. This verse is not merely a guiding suggestion—it is a command to all husbands about how to treat their wives. Our over-all goal must be to love our wives as Christ loves His church. This means we must be willing to lay down our life for her that she may rise up to the fullness of her potential in God.

Feminists may not appreciate the implications of this but God has so structured the marriage relationship that His love for His bride is revealed in the healthy love of a man for His wife. She rises to her greatest potential in such an environment of sacrificial love. The end result is an earthly picture of the relationship Christ has with His bride. This is why marriage is so close to the heart of God.

During this cancer challenge Mary has been a faithful caregiver to me. She has never complained about the many things she has to do that I am too weak for. She just keeps faithfully serving me day after day with faithful commitment. I have been truly humbled by her willingness to lay down her life for me during my struggle against cancer.

I wanted to have the Lord's perspective on the integral part Mary has played in my life. "Lord," I began. "I have been blessed with the most wonderful wife a man could ever desire. She is beautiful in spirit, soul and body and I am more in love with her than I ever thought possible. Tell me how you made her part of my life."

"Destiny" the Lord replied, "is a difficult concept for those who live in the natural plain. It is hard for many to understand how I could have been so involved in your lives that I could actually orchestrate things in such a way that the two of you finally end up in the same town, meet, and begin a relationship that leads to marriage and a life together.

"This is not difficult for the One by whom 'all things were created in heaven and on earth, visible and invisible, whether thrones or rulers or authorities or powers' (Col. 1:16). If I can number the hairs on your head and know when a sparrow falls, I am able to be involved in your lives according to My destiny for you."

"Jesus," I broke in, "It seems that the suffering of this cancer ordeal has actually strengthened Mary and helped her to rise up into her fullness as a person and child of God."

"My strength is perfected in weakness," the Lord responded. "When I spoke these words to Paul, he was hoping for a different response from Me. He was facing many situations where the enemy was attacking and he wanted freedom from these situations of weakness. But I was using them to perfect My strength in his life. As he allowed himself to be weak My strength was increased and completed in his life."

The Lord paused for a moment looking over at me with a comforting smile. Then he continued, "Mary has experienced the same thing. In this present weakness My strength in her has increased. She is becoming the woman of strength and spiritual power I destined her to be."

"I know that when we first married she did not think too highly of herself and at times was bothered by my assertive personality," I said.

"I will only speak to you about Mary in relation to how she affected your life. She and I will have our personal, private time here at the judgment seat. At that time I will help her understand how her life unfolded and how My grace helped her to blossom as a daughter of the King."

The Lord paused to let that last statement sink into my thinking. It was apparent that He would withhold things that needed to be discussed between just the two of them. On the other hand He wanted me to know how my life had affected hers and how hers had affected mine.

Then He continued, "It took you a while to realize that you were an integral part of Mary's life. My people sometimes do not understand that their destinies involve associations with others. You are not to live isolated lives apart from association with key people that I put in your lives. Mary and you were destined to walk much of your lives together and each of you would contribute to the fulfilling of each other's destiny."

That statement caught me a bit off guard. I had been thinking of my destiny as my personal calling that had nothing to do with anyone else. Now I was hearing from Jesus that our destinies often intersect with others and that we each play a part in the outworking of God's calling for our lives. His plan is not just for our individual lives but for integration with others he has destined to be part of our lives. This was exciting news.

Jesus continued, "I put Mary into your life for a purpose and I put you into her life for a purpose as well. Each of you was called to help the other reach the fullness of their destiny. In some ways Mary was weak in the flesh and you were strong in the flesh. I used Mary to chip away at your natural strength and I used you to help her open to My strength and realize it in her life."

"I was not much help to her in the early years of our marriage. I was so egotistical and sure of myself. I spent many of those early days trying to understand why she wouldn't just abandon her weakness and become strong like me," I said.

"My people," said Jesus, "until they mature, usually judge the lives of others with their own life as the standard. They make the mistake of thinking that the way they are is the way everyone should be. You made that mistake in regard to Mary. The result was that you deepened her lack of confidence and did little to help her see herself in God."

The Lord had just touched a sensitive chord in my life. I began to weep as I remembered those days of insensitivity on my part. I couldn't see past my own ego to embrace the needs of my bride. Tears flowed as I relived those days.

"These are good tears," the Lord continued as He nodded His approval. "They are tears that come from past repentance. Just remember that those years are under My blood and forgiven forever. But you are candid enough to see how you fell short of My best for you in those days. Such is the nature of spiritual growth toward maturity. You must crawl before you can walk and each step of your journey makes way for the next as you grow toward completeness in Me."

The Lord's words of admonition were like salve on a wound. I was immediately calmed by the knowledge that He knew and understood. Also, He always seemed to be forward-looking, expecting growth toward the appointed goal. His words brought comfort.

I now see that the greatest thing that has happened to me in my earthly journey is my marriage to Mary. Our times of weakness have caused her strength in God to rise to the surface. She is anything but a weak person at this point in our lives. Her spiritual strength is apparent to all who meet her. She has allowed God's sufficient grace to perfect His strength in her life. It is wonderful to see her rise to her position in Christ.

Our love has grown in wonderful ways. If love can be measured in terms of laying down one's life for another I can say that my life is poured out for her. This, of course, has been God's doing. He has used the attacks of cancer to allow my flesh to be weakened so that His strength could be perfected in me. This new strength is different from the old. It is tempered with the humility that comes with weakness. It flows completely from God, not my natural soul.

Jesus told his disciples, "Unless you become as little children, you will never enter the kingdom of heaven" (Matt. 18:3). I believe that Mary and I are becoming more like little children in many ways. The weakness in our lives has destroyed the pretense that comes with age and released the free, "I don't care what others think" spirit of the child. Saying, "I love you," has become as natural as breathing and the tender hug has become an essential part of every day.

I am so blessed to have the Mary that God destined—the Mary who sees herself through His eyes and not mine—the Mary who knows who she is in God and will not back down from that knowledge. This is the Mary God has perfected before my very eyes through the wonder of His grace. She honors me as she would Christ and treats me with the respect due a king. I am a blessed man.

And the icing on the cake is that she sure looks pretty in the morning light.

✝ Chapter 23: Prayer

I am blessed to be surrounded by people who pray. On two occasions, before my chemo-therapy treatment I called some of my brothers and sisters to come over the night before to pray for me. I am convinced that their prayer helped to keep my body from being devastated by the chemicals. They were faithful to come and hold me up before the Lord. I will always remember their love and kindness.

Prayer is a crucial part of the life of a follower of Christ. I have an earthly viewpoint of this great spiritual experience, but I wanted to see it from heaven's perspective. I broached the subject with a simple question of the Lord, "Jesus, would you explain prayer from your heavenly viewpoint?"

Consenting, the Lord said, "If you are expecting some sophisticated answer you may be disappointed. Prayer is simply communication with Me. It is a spirit to Spirit connection that enables My people to remain in spiritual union with their God."

"I see that Lord," I responded, "But aren't there different kinds of prayer designed to meet different needs?"

"A better way of looking at it is to see that there are times when communication with God must be intensified or directed to meet a particular need. In my earthly walk I was in constant communication with the Father. I only did what I saw the Father doing. It was necessary for Me to remain in continuing fellowship with Him. But there were times when a special need required an intensified communion with Him.

"When I was about to select My twelve apostles I spent the night in prayer. This was a crucial time in My ministry. I was about to choose the twelve men who would be responsible for carrying on My ministry after I was gone. My choices had to be the Father's choices.

"I also faced the dilemma of knowing that one of those I would choose would betray Me. I had to be clear on these choices so even though I was in continuing communion with the Father I went to the mountain all night to intensify and deepen our communion because of this important decision."

There was a holy seriousness in the Lord's demeanor as He explained this event. It was obvious that He took this subject very seriously and would want His people to understand it as well. I listened very carefully.

The Lord continued saying, "The form prayer takes depends on the situation. When I prayed for My church in the upper room I was prophetically proclaiming My purpose for the church age. I called for their oneness and for their protection. I knew I was going to the cross and I wanted to declare in prayer My Father's will that they receive the same glory that He had given to Me. The destiny of My church was encompassed in My words."

The Lord paused for a moment and let out a deep sigh. As I looked at Him His eyes reflected a sad tenderness. I knew that He was contemplating something ominous in nature.

"But," He continued, "in the Garden of Gethsemane I prayed a different kind of prayer. This prayer came from the agony of My soul over My impending crucifixion. It was a prayer that sought a clear, unmistakable word from the Father. I cried out, 'Father, if it is your will, take this cup from me. Nevertheless not My will, but yours be done' (Luke 22: 42). Even though an angel came to comfort Me, I agonized greatly over the decision that lay before Me. I had it within My power to avoid the cross but I knew how significant it was to the Father's plan."

Jesus paused but it was not a time for me to speak. We often forget that Jesus, though He existed as God, was fully human during His earthly ministry. He got tired like we all do. He experienced the sadness and hurt we all feel. The agony leading up to the cross and its pain were humanly real. His death was a real death, not something make-believe or pretend. His prayer in Gethsemane reflected that human reality.

Shifting the direction of the conversation, the Lord said, "Paul taught you to 'pray without ceasing' and to 'pray at all times in the Spirit' (1 Thess. 5:17; Eph. 6:18). He was exhorting you to remain in communion with God throughout the moments of the day. But He also recognized the need for special intensified prayer at certain times."

When Jesus mentioned "praying at all times in the Spirit" I thought of the context of that passage. Ephesians chapter six is about spiritual warfare against the demonic forces of the enemy. Here Paul admonishes us to put on the armor of God and realize that we are not fighting against flesh and blood but against the evil spiritual forces of Satan (vv. 11, 12). Of course this would call for a more intensified, warring prayer.

Jesus could tell where my thoughts had gone. He did not hesitate to agree with them: "Yes indeed! That passage calls for war prayer. Paul said, 'Take up the helmet of salvation, and the sword of the Spirit, which is the word of God, praying at all times with all prayer and petition in the Spirit, being watchful to this end...' This is obviously a call to prayer that wields the word of God as the sword of the Spirit in battle. It calls for petition for one's warring comrades and the need for a watchful, battle-ready vigilance."

I interjected, "This is the prayer attitude we must have to storm the gates of hell and extend God's kingdom."

"Yes," the Lord continued, "My bride must at times put on her combat boots and fight the fight of faith and prayer is an integral part of that process."

I have recounted how at one point in my treatment my bladder filled up with blood, blocking my urinary flow. After extensive treatment during three days in the hospital I finally came home from the ordeal. That day Mary and I were devastated to find blood in my urine once again. We could only imagine having to return to the hospital for more debilitating treatment.

My brother in Jesus, Dan, came over that afternoon at the leading of the Holy Spirit. Mary and I had been discussing how we believed that God wanted to change the way we prayed. I had been on the phone with Timm, another brother, who had shared the same thing. God was encouraging us to pray positive aggressive prayers according to His word and bind Satan and his forces instead of sheepishly begging Him.

Timm refers to this kind of prayer as "Canaan prayer" because it is battling prayer by which we take the ground God has given to us. He had given the land to the nation of Israel but they were required to go into the land and take it by military force. In the wilderness God simply met their needs but in the land of promise they were required to take by faith what He had promised.

War prayer is like that. It is not begging or even asking God for things but confidently coming against spiritual forces of evil to defeat them in His name. Once we have ascertained the will of God in a matter, we are to command His will into the situation.

Dan came with that kind of attitude that afternoon and prayed warring, Canaan prayer over my body. He commanded the blood issue to be healed and rebuked it in the name of Jesus. I went to bed confident that my body was healed. The next morning my urine was clear and the problem did not exist. Praise God for war prayer.

Continuing my conversation with Jesus, I asked a question that many have asked me. "Lord what does the expression praying 'in the spirit' mean?"

In response the Lord said, "Praying in the Spirit is prayer that originates in your human spirit under the inspiration of My Holy Spirit. It is praying with God as the Spirit leads. It can be praying in the spiritual language that I give to My people. When you are praying in this spiritual language you are crying out to God not necessarily knowing what you are saying, but the Holy Spirit is inspiring it and the result is prayer that hits the mark of God's will. The resulting confirmation in your spirit will verify this.

"But in this case the words 'praying in the Spirit' simply identify the origin of all true prayer. It is not flowing from one's mind but originating in the spirit and then being expressed in the mind and through the mouth. Since prayer is communion with God, who is Spirit, it must originate in your human spirit.

"Remember what I told the Samaritan woman at Jacob's well: 'God is Spirit and those who worship Him must worship in spirit and truth' (John 4: 24). It is impossible to worship a spiritual God through fleshly activity. Attempts to worship God apart from the spirit result in religion. The woman at the well wanted to argue with me about which mountain we should worship in. She was caught up in external concerns that ignored spirit to Spirit communion with God.

"The spirit of man is the lamp of the Lord. Only the fire of God's presence ignites the human spirit. The light that is produced brings spiritual clarity and vision. Prayer is the communion that comes from that union of human spirit and Holy Spirit. It is God touching man and man touching God."

"Lord," I broke in, "I have not seen prayer in this way. To see it from your divine viewpoint reveals how important prayer is. It is not just a ritual of words but a real communion between man and God through the Spirit. I will never see prayer the same."

"I'm glad to hear that," the Lord responded. "The Book of Revelation contains a passage which should help you grasp fully the importance of prayer. Before the sounding of the seven trumpets the angel mingled the incense with the prayers of the saints upon the heavenly altar. The smoke ascended to God. God's will is represented by the incense. It is mingled with the prayers of the saints and rises to God. Fire from the altar is then placed in the censer and thrown to the earth and the seven angels prepared themselves to sound their trumpets."

I began to think out loud at this point. "The incense and the prayers. God's Spirit and the spirit of man. All mingled with the fire of the altar. The fire is thrown to the earth and this event sets the stage for the seven trumpets."

I had read this passage many times. Now in the presence of the Lord I was seeing that our prayers, when combined with God's will actually move the hand of the angels and instigate the will of heaven. I recalled Jesus' words in the Lord's Prayer, "Your will be done on earth as it is in heaven" (Matt. 6:10). Our prayer brings the will of heaven to earth. Our cooperation with the will of heaven unleashes its effects upon the earth in situations in our lives. Through such prayer the kingdom of darkness is defeated and the kingdom of heaven extended.

Jesus had the last word on this matter: "Prayer is simply entering into communion with God and expressing the unity of that communion. It is man working with God to express His will upon the earth. The situation will determine the intensity of prayer. Pray without ceasing, but be ready always to pray with God's purpose and passion."

Indeed that was the final word on prayer. Jesus has a way of putting issues to rest with His simple explanations. He unveils heaven's perspective but always in simple, easy to understand words. I am blessed to be here with Him.

† Chapter 24: The Physical Appearance of Jesus

When I have shared these conversations with people often I am asked about what Jesus looked like. For some reason it seemed inappropriate to dwell on Jesus' physical features. I found myself hesitating when asked about His appearance. I broached this subject with the Lord for clarification.

"Lord, I have been asked by people to explain what you look like." I began. "For some reason I am hesitant to get into detail about your physical appearance. How should I handle such questions?"

Jesus smiled with that big smile and nodded His head back and forth as I asked my question. He was obviously amused by it.

"And what have you told them when they asked," He inquired.

Somewhat embarrassed I replied, "I have told them that you appear as a normal man with a clean-shaven face, short dark hair and a simple robe. Your skin is darker than mine and your face and eyes are like many other people I have seen. I try to explain that you appear in every way as a normal man."

Jesus didn't seem eager to venture into this subject. He simply smiled with a wonderful twinkle in His eyes and looked over at me as if waiting for me to continue.

"One dear sister asked me if you had penetrating eyes," I said.

"And how did you respond to that question?" the Lord asked.

"I said that your physical eyes seemed quite normal to me, but there was definitely something penetrating about your presence. You seem to see right through me and know my thoughts and motives. My heart seems to be an open book to you. And yet I am comfortable in your presence because your penetrating heart is without condemnation."

After a brief pause the Lord simply began to quote a passage from Hebrews: "For the word of God is living and powerful, sharper than any two-edged sword, piercing to the division of soul and spirit, of joints and marrow, and discerning the thoughts and intentions of the heart. And no creature is hidden from His sight, but all are naked and exposed to the eyes of Him to whom we must give account" (Heb. 4:12, 13).

Jesus waited for a moment as if to say that the words from Hebrews speak for themselves. Indeed they did but I still wanted to hear more.

Abruptly He said, "I am the Word of God. With My spiritual eyes I am able to penetrate and separate between soul and spirit, between the external and the internal. I am able to discern the thinking and motives of the heart. It is impossible to hide from Me because everything is an open book to Me."

I was quick to reply to this. "Lord, that's exactly the way I feel in your presence. It's as if you know not only what I am thinking but why I am thinking it. And yet I am not threatened by this penetration of your spiritual eyes. Instead, it is a comfort to me."

"But," I continued, "this has nothing to do with your physical appearance. Your physical eyes are quite normal but your spiritual eyes penetrate into the heart."

Picking up this thought the Lord said, "You will find virtually nothing in My word about My physical appearance. This was by design. First of all, the physical appearance means nothing. Secondly, I knew that the fleshly tendency of men would be to make icons of My image and worship them.

"Idolatry is a tendency of the fallen human heart. In the Commandments I said, 'You shall not make any carved image of any likeness of anything that is in heaven above.' It is My concern that people will try to make an image of Me to worship instead of drawing near to me in person."

Remembering what Paul said about this I said, "I remember Paul's admonition, 'Therefore, from now on, we regard no one according to the flesh. Even though we have known Christ according to the flesh, yet now we know Him thus no longer' (2 Cor. 5:16). Paul was saying that we should know people not according to their fleshly characteristics but according to their hearts. The disciples had known you in the flesh but now they were to leave that fleshly understanding and know you by the Spirit."

Jesus nodded his approval of what I had said. After a short moment of silence He responded, "Peoples' concerns about My physical appearance are misguided. This reflects a human tendency to judge by the external instead of what is inside a person. Apart from the scars that I bear in My body, I have nothing to offer people through My physical appearance. It is who I am that really matters. Encourage people to seek to know Me, not to know about Me. In knowing Me you will not be concerned about My physical appearance."

At this moment, though I know the Lord did not mean it that way, I felt a little like I had been given a gentle scolding. Perhaps I was feeling this in behalf of others I know who have these concerns about the Lord's physical appearance. The Hollywood renditions of Jesus are often so removed from historical truth that we have been misguided concerning what He looked like. He was, after all, a Hebrew man who had worked all His life as a carpenter in Nazareth. Somehow Hollywood always finds a way to portray Him in its own image. That, I believe, is a serious mistake.

If we are concerned with the appearance of our Lord, perhaps the description in the Book of Revelation is more appropriate. The apostle John saw "One like the Son of Man, clothed with a garment down to the feet and girded about the chest with a golden band. His head and hair were white like wool, as white as snow, and His eyes like a flame of fire. His feet were like fine brass, as if refined in a furnace, and His voice as the sound of many waters. He had in His right hand seven stars, out of His mouth went a sharp two-edged sword and His countenance was like the sun shining in full strength. And when I saw Him, I fell at His feet as dead" (Rev. 1:13-17).

With all of its symbolic significance, this is a description of Jesus that shows Him as He is. When I first met Him at the judgment seat, my knees buckled and I fell to my knees, not because of what He looked like but because of who He is. Now, by the Spirit, we can be present with Him at all times concerned only with the penetrating power of His presence.

† Chapter 25: Becoming a Bondservant of the Lord

Paul and some of the other apostles referred to themselves as bondservants of the Lord. Peter, James and Jude use this word of their relationship to the Lord, and Epaphras is called a bondservant by Paul. The Greek word that is used really refers to a slave.

The Book of Exodus gives strict instructions about slaves and how they are to be treated. A bondservant was obligated to serve his master for six years but in the seventh year he was allowed to be free. The bondservant could choose to give up his freedom and stay with his master for the rest of his life. In this case his ear would be pierced with an awl as a symbol that he belonged to the master forever (Ex. 21:2-6). Having made this choice he was the possession of the master from that point on and the master would take care of his food, lodging and clothing and other needs.

When the disciples called themselves bondservants of the Lord they were speaking from this background of Hebrew history. Even in the early days of the church this form of master-slave relationship was practiced (Col. 4:1). They knew the significance of calling themselves bondservants of the Lord. They had given up their freedom to become bondservants of the Lord for life. He had placed His mark on them and they belonged to Him.

I wondered how the Lord felt about all of this. I know that if Paul and the other disciples saw themselves as bondservants of the Lord that the Lord as their Master would have a fresh, divine perspective.

"Lord, what does it mean to be your bondservant?" I asked.

Jesus looked at me with an expression I had not seen before. He took in a deep breath as He tilted His head back and forward again and closed His eyes in thought.

Then He began replying, "As you have noticed, Paul and the others use the word 'bondservant' of themselves. This commitment came from within their hearts. The bondservant has the choice of freedom from servanthood or a lifetime of committed service to Me. They reached a point where they knew that their lives did not belong to them but were sacrificed to serve Me. They knew that they were bought with a price and had committed to serve Me fully."

"Lord, aren't all Christians your bondservants?" I asked.

"Sadly, no," the Lord replied. "Many choose their freedom rather than a lifetime of service to Me. Many have left their first love and have allowed the world to capture their hearts. Many have chosen to serve other gods of wealth and pleasure. In many cases their spiritual life has been choked out by the cares of this world. No, all are not My bondservants!"

"It seems like a very serious commitment to give up one's life to become your servant for life," I replied. "This would mean forsaking one's personal goals and relying totally upon you for life's needs."

"I am familiar with this commitment," He went on. "I too was a bondservant of the Father during My earthly life. Paul said of Me, "He emptied Himself, taking on the form of a bondservant, and coming in the likeness of men" (Phil. 2:7). I was a bondservant to My Father.

"I emptied Myself of My personal desires and gave Myself fully to Him for His will. I only did what the Father told Me to do. I did not act on My own but obeyed the Father in all things. I was His bondservant. My obedience led Me to the cross. I humbled myself and became obedient to death, even the death of the cross."

I sheepishly replied, "So you were a bondservant as well?"

"Indeed I was," He replied. "From the moment I was led into the wilderness by the Spirit, I became a bondservant of the Father. Much of the message I brought was to be seen in the life that I lived."

"Your life example was your message," I responded, seeking clarification.

"Obedience is better than sacrifice. A life lived has more power than words. Words without life are empty and powerless," came His response.

Jesus paused for a moment while the words made their way into my thinking.

"My people," He continued, "often think that words and external activities are the evidence of spirituality. The only real evidence of godliness is a life lived in submission to God. I showed people how to live through the life that I lived. A bondservant is one who lives His life under direction from Me. They give themselves to Me as I gave Myself to the Father."

After a long contemplative pause I said, "Lord, I want to be your bondservant."

"This is not a decision that I make but one that comes from your own heart," He responded. "You must count the cost and decide if you can put your hand to the plow without looking back."

"Yes, Lord," was all that I could say for I knew that I had not fully counted the cost. I see that decision on my horizon. I know that it is a life that must be lived daily. May God give me grace to make the right decision.

† Chapter 26: Divine Healing

My friend and brother in Christ, Tom, came by on a couple of occasions to visit me in the hospital. We had fellowship and played some games of cribbage. His back had been hurting him for several years and he was unable to do some of the simplest things.

As we fellowshipped one day the subject of divine healing came up. We talked about some verses from the word such as Isaiah 53 and Psalm 103:1-3 that speak of God's healing power. I shared with him some stories of people I had seen healed. A young former student of mine, for example, had been miraculously healed of cystic fibrosis as we prayed for her. We openly discussed these events and the passages of scripture.

As Tom was leaving he said, "Lloyd if you are ever of a mind to do so, I would love it if you would pray for my back."

I said I would be happy to do so as he opened the door and said goodbye. As he walked out the door I said a quiet prayer for his healing.

Later, Tom related how the Lord had totally healed his back. He had no more pain and was able to do many things that he had not been able to do before. We were all excited to hear this and rejoiced with him. I believe that Tom, in our time together simply opened his heart to God's healing power and God quietly healed his body.

There was a time in my ministry when divine healing was common. People with bone problems were virtually always healed. This young lady was healed of cystic fibrosis, an incurable disease. Another lady who had been in a serious accident came to us with a seriously misaligned spine. She was going in the next day to have her neck vertebrae fused. She walked with a noticeable limp from a displaced hip. Much of her spine was out of place and she was in excruciating pain.

When we prayed for her she was completely healed from head to toe. People witnessed her muscles rippling and her bones popping as the Holy Spirit healed her body. Her hip was realigned by the power of God. She was healed and came to Christ that night in a mighty way. Many other stories could be recounted in which people were healed.

But there came a time when it was as if God removed His healing hand from my ministry. This came during the time when I inadvertently began to take credit for the wonderful things going on in the church. I allowed the success of the church and the accolades of people to go to my head and I allowed God's glory to be reflected to me.

When God began to reprimand me for my behavior He said, "You're not going there!" He was not going to allow Me to go down that road of religious disobedience.

I remember after that time praying for many people but none of them were obviously healed. I prayed for a brother's back one evening and instead of being healed he spun in circles. It was as if God was saying, "I'm still here but I'm not healing through your hands at this time." During this time God led us into a time of wilderness dealings that are recounted in another part of this narrative. God had apparently removed His healing hand from my ministry for reasons that I was to learn later.

Since that time I have fought three battles against cancer. I am in the middle of one of those battles as I write. For His own reasons the Lord has chosen not to miraculously heal my body but has allowed me to go through conventional medical treatment. I am in a place where I need serious clarification from God on the subject of His healing power.

Last night I broached the issue with the Lord. I asked, "Jesus, I am not clear concerning divine healing. It seems that in recent years I have become less and less clear as I have not seen healing in my ministry and have had serious medical problems in my own life. I need to know how you feel about this subject."

The Lord was nodding His head in apparent approval of the question. He pursed His lips and squinted His eyes as He thought out His answer.

"During My earthly ministry," He began, "I revealed God's will through the things that I said and did. I had come to do the will of My Father. If people will study my ministry and take note of how I conducted Myself, they will see God's will revealed."

"I remember what Peter told Cornelius about your healing ministry," I replied. "He said of you: 'God anointed Jesus of Nazareth with the Holy Spirit and with power. He went about doing good and healing all who were oppressed by the devil, because God was with Him' (Acts 10:38). That says it all."

"I came to destroy the works of the devil and to empower My followers to do the same" He continued. "Wherever I went I healed the sick and diseased, cast out demons, raised the dead and proclaimed the good news of the kingdom. I brought God's kingdom into the situations I faced by releasing God's will into them."

As the Lord paused I responded, "From what you're saying there seems to be no doubt that it is God's will to heal the sick."

"Sin and sickness," He went on," "are the two main devastations of the enemy. These are twin evils, one affecting the spirit of man and the other his body. Satan was out to destroy man spiritually and physically. I came to destroy His works and empower My people to follow in My steps."

"The prophet Isaiah spoke of your twofold ministry," I said. "He prophesied of you, 'Surely He has borne our diseases and carried our afflictions. So we esteemed Him stricken, beaten by God, and afflicted. But He was wounded for our transgression, crushed for our iniquities and upon Him was the punishment that brought us peace for with His stripes we are healed'" (Isa. 53:4, 5).

"Yes," Jesus replied. "Matthew quoted parts of this passage when recounting how I healed all who were sick. He said, 'He healed all who were sick, that it might be fulfilled which was spoken by Isaiah the prophet, saying, "He himself took our infirmities and bore our sicknesses."' My ministry was based upon the work of the cross which would be fulfilled when I gave My life for all. There I bore the sin and sickness for all humanity."

"Sin and sickness seem to be like twin tools of the enemy," I volunteered.

"Indeed they are," Jesus continued. "I remember the time the friends of a paralyzed man broke through the roof of the house we were in to let him down into the house. When I saw their faith I said, 'Son, your sins are forgiven you.' Some scribes who were there were offended that I would forgive sins as a remedy for his paralysis.

"I replied to them, 'Which is easier, to say to the paralytic, 'Your sins are forgiven you,' or to say, 'Arise, take up your bed and walk'? Then I looked them in the eye and said, 'But that you may know that the Son of Man has power on earth to forgive sins…I say to you, arise, take up your bed and go to your house.' Of course, the man was healed and walked out on his own power" (Mark 2:3-12).

"So you demonstrated that sin and sickness go hand in hand." I replied excitedly. "You forgave the man's sin and healed His body in one motion. When you healed his body his sins were forgiven. Or it could be said that you forgave him by healing his body."

"I bore both sickness and disease on the cross,." the Lord replied. "Both of these weapons of the enemy were destroyed."

'Lord, if that is true and I know it is, why is it that some people are not healed?" I asked.

He shook His head positively and smiled as if He had anticipated the question. Then He said, "There are conditions to My healing power. Remember when I was in Nazareth I did not do many mighty works because of their unbelief. In an atmosphere of unbelief the release of God's supernatural power is hindered.

"In the United States, for example, there is such an atmosphere of unbelief that I am not able to do many mighty works. In China and Africa and other places I am able to do mighty works through My people because they believe that I am able."

I realized immediately the truth in what Jesus said. We both sat in the silence for a moment knowing that He had more to say on this subject.

After a pause He said, "Another condition to My healing power is the presence of My body. The context of My supernatural works is the unified body of Christ. Did I not say 'Where two of you agree on earth concerning anything that you shall ask, it shall be done for you by My Father in heaven'?

"Further, I said, 'For where two or three are gathered together in My name, I am there in their midst.' These words are spoken in the context of My exhortations to the people concerning life in My body. When I am the guest of honor among you the church is present. When the church is present there is agreement in Me by the Spirit. This agreement allows you to ask according to My will and My Father will give what you ask."

I replied, "I know this to be true Lord, but so many of your people see the body of Christ as composed of all Christians, regardless of their condition."

The Lord replied quickly, "Of course we've touched on this before but let Me repeat this important truth. The body of Christ is not just a loosely piled stack of building stones. It takes shape when those stones are placed next to one another for the building of a dwelling place. The church is the dwelling place of God on earth. He lives in each saint but He dwells in the midst of the church."

"Lord," I replied, "Most Christians believe that they are automatically a part of the church when they are saved."

"When they are saved they become building material for My church. They are in the church only when they present themselves to be placed into My spiritual temple according to My will. The church is 'the called out ones.' To be called out one must hear Me calling and answer the call to come out to Me. Those who come to Me gather in My name and become the church."

The Lord paused to let this sink in. His words answered many questions for Me. Jesus had promised that He would build His church and "the gates of hell would not prevail against it" (Matt. 16: 18). The church is God's people storming the gates of hell. It seems to me that much of what we call the church is being stormed by the gates of hell, the reverse of what Christ promised. The church, then, must be something bigger then we understand.

Paul had declared in Ephesians that the Father, "Put all things under His feet, and gave Him as head over all things to the church, which is His body, the fullness of Him who fills all in all." This incredible statement makes it clear that what God calls the church is the expression of His fullness. In other words when people see the church on earth they should see God manifest, for the body of Christ is His fullness.

Men define the church much more loosely than God does. If Christians do not present themselves to God for His eternal purpose, they remain isolated believers disconnected from the church. When we present our bodies to Him for His purpose He is able to build us into His church which expresses His life on earth.

Knowing My thoughts the Lord interjected His own: "That expression of My body is the context in which I am able to do many mighty works. Notice the result of the body life My early followers were experiencing. Luke wrote, 'Then fear came upon every soul, and many wonders and signs were done through the apostles' (Acts 2:43). When My body is in place functioning as I designed it, I am able to move in power in the midst of the resulting unity and love."

"So again," I replied, "It comes down to the healthy church functioning as you designed it. In that context of unity you are able to heal the sick and do other mighty works through your people. If we are truly gathered in your name and agreeing with your will you come into our midst just as you did during your earthly ministry."

"Yes," He responded, "I said, 'He who believes in Me, will also do the works that I do; and greater works then these shall he do because I am going to My Father' (John 14:12). In going to My Father I was preparing to pour out My Spirit upon My people to empower My church to continue to do what I had been doing. They would do greater works than I had done because My Holy Spirit was upon them producing the body of Christ, the place of My power."

I had read about the Christians in places like China who had been forced by persecution to come together in the unity and love of the body Christ. Because they were functioning as the body of Christ signs and wonders were part of their experience. The functioning of the unified, loving body of Christ provides the context in which Christ can move in power and thus heal the sick.

In the western world Christians have abandoned the real expression of the body of Christ for an individualized Christianity. We have partitioned ourselves into many factions and wonder why God does not move in our midst. There is no gray area allowed in the matter of being a Christian. We are either followers of Christ or we are doing our own thing. True followers of Christ will come together as the body of Christ. There is no in-between. In America we have chosen the gray area and that is the primary reason why God does not visit us in power.

Paul wrote, "Now to him who is able to do much more abundantly than all we ask or think, according to the power working within us, to Him be glory in the church and in Christ Jesus throughout all generations, forever and ever" (Eph. 3:20, 21). God is able to do amazing things according to the power working in us but we must not lose track of the words "in the church."

Paul speaks of this same power in the first chapter of Ephesians. He says that it is the "Power toward us who believe, according to the working of His great might that He worked in Christ when He raised Him from the dead and seated Him at His right hand" (Eph. 1:19, 20).

But Paul ends with this declaration that Christ is "...far above all rule and authority and power and dominion, and above every name that is named, not only in this age but in the one to come. And He put all things under His feet and gave Him as head over all things to the church, which is His body, the fullness of Him who fills all in all" (vv. 21-23).

There is nothing ambivalent about this verse. It declares to us that Christ, to whom has been given all power, is Head over the church, the fullness of God. God's power has been given to the church, the body of Christ. He is seated in the heavenlies at the right hand of the Father, but He has given His power to His church.

The Lord wasn't finished with His answer to my question. "My people must remember that I am the sovereign God. Paul rightly said of Me, 'For He says to Moses, "I will have mercy on whomever I will have mercy, and I will have compassion on whomever I will have compassion...Therefore He has mercy on whom He wills, and whom He wills He hardens'" (Rom. 9:15-18).

"My answer to those who question My judgment is 'But indeed, O man, who are you to reply against God? Will the thing formed say to him who formed it, "Why have you made me like this?" Does not the potter have power over the clay, for the same lump to make one vessel for honor and another for dishonor?'" (Rom. 9:20, 21).

The Lord paused for a moment as if to give me a chance to respond. I did not think this was an appropriate moment for me to say anything. The Lord had the floor and it was His to keep at this point.

"Always remember," He went on, "that I dwell in eternity. I see beyond your ability to see. I make decisions based upon my eternal vision. There are times when My people must simply be willing to submit to My sovereignty. I may choose not to heal someone because I know that in their future they will commit murder. I may choose not to heal someone because of what I know about their hearts. These are decisions to be left up to God and not questioned. The clay must not in ignorance question the potter."

Some weeks after this conversation with Jesus I lost a dear pastor friend of mine to cancer. John Kunz had been a pastor in our community for many years and his daughter Jennifer and my daughter Karis had been good friends in high school. I had visited John and prayed for him a few days before he went to be with Jesus. I remembered these words of the Lord about His sovereignty when I heard the news of John's death. We must be willing to submit to His sovereignty.

There was finality in this statement by Jesus. My question had been thoroughly answered and at this point I certainly felt like I was the clay and Jesus was the Potter. I nodded my thanks to the Lord and He smiled back His "You're welcome."

† Chapter 27: My Commission: Tear Down that Wall

Throughout these encounters with Jesus at the judgment seat He has revealed to me key elements of the future revival of the church. I have learned that there will be a rising up of the church in my lifetime. This rising up of the church will set the stage for an end time church which will ultimately join the Lamb of God and His angels in defeating Satan and his demonic horde. How soon this will happen has not been revealed to me. For some reason the Lord stays away from giving the time frame of these future events.

As I consider the significance of these revelations I wonder what my part is. What is the Lord calling me to do with this knowledge and the eagerness He has created in my heart to do His will? A simple question of the Lord brought the answer.

"I wonder what my part is in all of this Lord." I asked. "You've filled my heart with revelation about your church so I can't help but wonder what you want me to do with it."

"There is a wall of tradition that halts this revival," He began, "and that wall must be penetrated before this revival can break loose. I am calling you and many others to teach, preach and live the truth about My eternal purpose until the wall is penetrated and eventually brought down. In so doing you pave the way for a new expression of the church."

"I have encountered this wall before," I responded. "Wherever I have gone in the organized church I have been met with fierce opposition due to the entrenchment of strong traditions. It seems as though a veil lies over the spiritual eyes of those who are heavily committed to the established church."

A look of faraway sadness entered His face as Jesus gazed at the heavenly horizon. "How quickly My people have set aside My word for the sake of their traditions! How easily they are removed from the simplicity of the gospel for the sake of their religious notions! Each time I have sought to bring revival to My church I have had to find men and women who were willing and able to take a stand against the engrained traditions of the day in order to enable Me to create a new wineskin for My revival wine."

Here we were again talking about the condition of organized Christianity and the simplicity of the new wineskin Christ desires to produce. It seems that all roads of conversation lead back to this subject. Without the existence of a functioning body of Christ nothing that the Lord has shared with me makes sense. With the body of Christ operating as God designed from the beginning, everything falls wonderfully into place.

"Another part of your commission," the Lord continued, "is to help the church know how to keep from falling back into tradition. You will be used to teach people to live in the present moment and day, being guided by My Holy Spirit. Traditions develop when men begin to live by what happened yesterday. I am new every day. My ways, like the manna in the wilderness, cannot be carried over to the next day. I will provide new manna every day for the day I have given. Live this and teach it to My people."

"Thank you, Lord, for helping me to see my place in your purpose." I said. "I am humbled to know that you have called me to a definite purpose in your will. But Lord I need your wisdom about how I am to go about this."

The Lord was quick to respond to this concern. "I have given you My Holy Spirit. He will guide you into My truth and reveal to you My ways as you daily seek Me. As you teach the people to live by the Spirit you must also become an example for them to follow. In My earthly ministry I only did what I saw the Father doing. I submitted to His will completely for My daily and momentary actions. You are to listen for the voice of the Holy Spirit in the same way. He will speak to you at all times revealing how to proceed in My will."

Each of us has a calling from God. He prepared works for us before He created the world. We were planned and purposed before the earth and the universe and everything was made for us. We are the center of God's creation, the reason for it all. Our challenge is to listen to Him and allow Him to reveal to us what we are called to accomplish for His purpose.

I used to envision myself preaching to large groups and traveling the world with the message God put within me. Now I know that more people are reached through the multiplication process of person to person ministry. The first disciples accomplished the worldwide spread of Christianity, not by preaching to throngs of people, although that occasionally happened, but by going where the Holy Spirit led and doing what He said.

The small group divisions of the early church were spiritual cells teeming with life. They transformed culture around them because they were among the people, in the streets and market places. They were truly the light of the world and the salt of the earth.

Although I hesitate to attempt to predict the future, I suppose that God is calling me to use my writing and teaching to spread the message of His eternal purpose. Person to person and in these small gatherings I will teach and exhort as He leads.

It is a difficult calling to break the barrier of tradition. I know from experience that it comes with much criticism and even persecution. It does not bring the accolades of established Christianity but is sure to bring their opposition. Nevertheless, that barrier must be broken, that wall must be brought down, if God is to have a way to bring His people into the fullness of His next renewal. That renewal may well be the beginning of His end time restoration of the true church.

If you are part of the organized church let me remind you that all of God's revivals of the past came with much opposition from the status quo. From the opposition that the Pharisees gave Jesus to the resistance of mainline churches to the charismatic revival, each renewal had to struggle against the traditions of the old wineskin being replaced. For the most part those old wineskins remain to this day containing the old stale religious wine of past days. God moves on but many choose not to move with Him.

Open your heart to God. Let Him give you spiritual vision to see what He is doing. As Paul wrote to the Ephesian church I pray "…that the God of our Lord Jesus Christ, the Father of glory, may give to you a spirit of wisdom and revelation in the full knowledge of Him, the eyes of your hearts being enlightened" (Eph. 1:17, 18). Let this new vision help you to look beyond the sacred cows of tradition and motivate you to return to a fresh, new exploration of God's word.

Let Him show you the simplicity of His church and how men have complicated it with fleshly offerings having no basis in God's word. Each generation brings its baggage along with it. It is time to repack our bags with new provisions for a new destination.

I envision small gatherings of people throughout our cities and in the rural areas coming together with Christ as the guest of honor. They will come together regularly to feast on God's word, the bread of life, and openly participate as the Spirit leads. Individuals will be built up in their faith and the corporate church will grow in unity and love. I see many of these groups gathering together on occasion for larger meetings that provide a setting for musical celebration and preaching of God's word by the equipping ministries.

I envision a slowly rising tide of inner-city ministry that sparks a multiplication of the church as these believers openly share their faith and lead others to Christ. The underground church will quietly burst forth with new life and growth.

These churches will need no pastor to organize and control them for the Holy Spirit will lead them into His truth. There will be many pastors ministering throughout the church as the Lord directs. They will need no large buildings because they will meet among the people in homes, in the parks, streets and marketplaces.

They will need no manmade programs to foster action, for the Holy Spirit will daily bring His program into their lives. They certainly will have no need of an evangelistic program because the very simple nature of the church will inspire an explosion of informal evangelism in the lives of the saints. Genuine love will attract the true seekers of God's life.

It is already happening. Ten years ago one heard virtually nothing about small group churches. No books were written on the subject. Now, many teachers of God's word have caught the vision and are openly teaching and writing about it.

An underground church is slowly arising from the chaos of the age. No doubt there will be false starts and phony imitations along the way, but through it all God will produce the new wineskin and pour out the new wine of His purpose. The beginning has begun and it will be exciting to see what the Lord does in the coming days.

† Chapter 28: The Condition of the Organized Church

One night I asked the Lord about the bride of Christ. Most Christians believe that the bride of Christ consists of all Christians. I have come to believe that the bride is a remnant of believers—a church within the church. I believe that the bride is composed of those who give themselves fully to Christ just as any bride would be wholly committed and faithful to her groom.

So I asked, "Lord there is a controversy concerning the identity of your bride. I know what many others believe and I know what I believe. Is your bride composed of all Christians or is she a select group chosen from within the church?"

The Lord waited for some time before He replied and His answer surprised me. "I cannot answer that question for you." And then He paused to consider my reaction

I replied, "Lord, you've answered every question I've asked so far and I know that you must have a special reason for holding back the answer to this one."

Jesus took in a deep breath and let it out. Slowly He crafted His reply.

He firmly began, "It is part of your destiny to discover that truth in My word for yourself so that you may teach it among My people. Approach My word the way you did when you sought the truth about salvation—with an open mind and a keen desire to know only truth. In so doing you will discover and know who comprises My bride. Your personal discovery of this truth in My word will prepare you to proclaim it to My people."

This was not the answer I expected. But we do not always get the answer we want from the Lord. He does not tickle our ears but consistently speaks truth. He is truth and can speak nothing less.

Then an amazing thing happened. How He did what He did I do not know. Suddenly, a collection of scriptures dropped into my thinking. I have some background in the study of God's word so it is not unusual for me to think of scriptures connected to certain issues. But this was a complete deposit of a large assortment of passages into my thought process. The passages seemed related at first glance but I would have to read and study them before I would see a connection. I looked forward to what I would find.

I began in the book of 1 Corinthians. I immediately was impressed with how much the condition of the church in that ancient Greek city resembled the spiritual condition of the structured church in modern day America.

First of all, I noticed the words in the first chapter, "For it has been reported to me by Chloe's household that there are contentions among you, my brethren. What I mean is that each one of you says, 'I am of Paul,' or 'I am of Apollos,' or 'I am of Cephas,' or 'I am of Christ'" (vv. 11, 12). The Corinthians were dividing from one another based upon their fleshly preferences of prominent teachers.

Paul represented those who preferred a knowledgeable, scholarly writer and teacher. Others preferred the fiery preacher Apollos with his eloquent preaching and charismatic ways. Some preferred the traditional Jewish approach of Peter. Still others, to differentiate themselves from the others were saying 'We are of Christ.' Paul wrote later that this denominational attitude was evidence that they were fleshly and not spiritual Christians (3: 3, 4).

The church in America is doing the same thing today. It has divided itself into groups named after its favorite teacher, doctrine or religious practice. Like the Corinthians, it proves its carnal condition by breaking up the body of Christ based on fleshly characteristics instead of walking by the Spirit. Instead of letting the Holy Spirit lead them into unity in Christ, they are allowing their fleshly preferences to divide the body of Christ.

It is even worse today because Christians separate into denominations and think it is normal. Indeed it is considered normal for Christians to break up the body of Christ, which is the expression of Christ on earth, for the sake of their fleshly inclinations. Somehow our positions about minor matters of doctrine have become more important than our unity with one another.

If you have joined with those who name themselves Presbyterians, or one of the other traditional churches, you follow in the footsteps of those in Corinth who said, "We are of Cephas." If you are part of a more contemporary church with an eloquent teacher you are of the same mind as those in Corinth who said, "We are of Apollos." If you prefer the teacher who is scholarly, a methodical Bible teacher, and a writer of books, you are in the "We are of Paul" camp.

God forbid that any of us should gather in honor of Christ and let Him, through the Spirit, lead us into His truth! Like the Corinthians, we prove our carnality by the factions that exist among us. In many cases we are not a people who walk according to the Spirit, but according to our personal fleshly desires. What a shame!

Next I looked at the third chapter of the epistle to the church in Corinth. Paul begins by calling them carnal Christians and offering the evidence that there were divisions among them (v. 3). He says, "…are you not carnal and walk like men?" They were following the inclinations of man rather than humbling themselves and committing to the will of God.

They were organizing into groups based upon how men felt instead of seeking and submitting to God's desires. No doubt they were making decisions based on expediency and practicality instead of asking God what He wanted to do.

Tragically this description fits the church in America like a glove. It is moved almost entirely by human expediency and practicality instead of the voice of God. Decisions are made in the same way a corporation committee makes decisions for its future. We are acting like mere men rather than redeemed followers of the living God.

In today's Christian climate much of this is taken for granted. Paul took this matter of division and carnality very seriously. When we jump down to verse ten we begin to see how seriously Paul takes it. He uses the analogy of a building to speak of the temple of God, His church. In so doing he says, "As a wise master builder I have laid the foundation, and another builds on it. But let every person take heed how he builds on it. For no other foundation can anyone lay than that which is laid, which is Jesus Christ" (1 Cor. 3:10, 11).

Paul says here that he had laid the foundation of the temple in the city of Corinth through his apostolic activity. Once the foundation is laid it becomes the responsibility of each follower of Christ to contribute to the building up of the corporate temple of God.

Paul explains the varying quality of the contributions we can make by saying, "If anyone builds on this foundation with gold, silver, precious stones, wood, hay, straw, each one's work will become clear" (v. 12, 13).

The apostle lists these building materials in descending order of value beginning with gold and ending with stubble. Silver is the second most valuable building material, precious stones are third, wood is fourth, and hay is fifth.

Of course the least valuable of these materials is stubble, the straw made from the leftover stalks after the harvesting of grain. Paul is implying that the Corinthian Christians through their carnal behavior were making worthless contributions to the building of God's temple. They were contributing to the man-made, destructible things of wood, hay and stubble, instead of the permanent, eternal things of God's making.

Their carnality was resulting in a temple that was of man and not of God. If a time of testing would come their materials would be destroyed because they were not durable but easily destructible.

Paul makes it clear that a time of judgment is coming which he refers to as "the Day." This Day of Judgment will come with the fire of God, which will test each person's work. Those who have built in the will of God with the materials provided by God will receive a reward for their efforts. Those who have built with man-made destructible material will suffer loss. They will be saved but their loss will be obvious.

I for one do not want to stand before the Lord at the judgment and hear Him say that He is not pleased with the works I have done. I want to hear the words, "Well done, good and faithful servant." How we build in the church is crucial to the judgment we will one day face. The materials we build with must be those He has chosen, not those we have chosen out of expediency or human cleverness.

In today's organized church many are building with the sub-par materials of human expediency and practicality. They are using the business methods of the world to build rather than the guidance of the Holy Spirit. The materials are not contributing to the lasting construction of God's temple on earth, the body of Christ.

They are building something but it does not contain the beauty, splendor and precious value of God. It has the stench of man's hands on it and the materials are cheap and second rate. Paul's admonition should be taken to heart: "Let each one take heed how he builds on it."

Christians are led to believe that the church is that big building on the corner with its eloquent pastor and clever programs. They are not taught that the church, the temple of God, is composed of people. It is the people of God coming together to answer the call of Christ on their lives. It is people allowing Christ to be the guest of honor in their gatherings.

Paul asks the important question that we should ask today: "Do you not know that you are the temple of God and that the Spirit of God dwells in you?" The pronoun "you" in this verse is plural, not singular. He is telling the Corinthians that together they form a local expression of the corporate temple of God.

The church of Jesus Christ is the temple of God on earth expressed in various localities. Paul reiterates this truth to the Ephesians where he wrote, "…all the building fitly joined together grows into a holy temple in the Lord, in whom you also are built together for a dwelling place of God in the Spirit" (Eph. 2:21, 22). We are the temple of the Holy Spirit and it is growing daily. How we contribute our part is serious business.

Dear church in America, do you realize that you are the dwelling place of God on earth? Do you realize the tremendous importance of how you build on the foundation that has been laid? Do you think God is going to honor your works when you have not consulted Him as to the materials? Most importantly of all, do you realize how this affects the heart of God?

These are serious questions that each of us must answer. There will come a Day of judgment fire, speaking spiritually, when our works will be judged in the fiery presence of the living God.

Let us take Paul's warning seriously: "Let each person take heed how he builds on it." Let us take heed concerning the works God has assigned to us concerning His church, the temple of God.

Next I opened the fifth chapter of 1 Corinthians. There Paul deals with the problem of immorality in the church. Paul wrote, "It is actually reported that there is sexual immorality among you and such sexual immorality as is not so much as named among the Gentiles, that one has his father's wife. And you are puffed up, and have not rather mourned, that he who has done this deed might be taken away from among you" (1 Cor. 5:1, 2).

The real problem in this situation is that the church was puffed up concerning this matter. They were so spiritually complacent that they did not realize the danger of allowing open, rebellious sin to exist within the church. They had grown callous to the presence of immorality in their midst and were even proud of their tolerant attitude.

The sin of Corinth pales in comparison to the immorality that today's church in America tolerates. Like Corinth we have grown callous to the presence of immorality among us. The divorce rate in the organized church is the same as that of the world. We thumb our nose at the divine institution that reflects God's eternal purpose. Pastors divorce the wives of their youth and are welcomed back into ministry with a new wife. We look at divorce and shrug our shoulders with complacent, puffed up attitudes that disregard the will of God.

Members of churches are living with one another in a state of adultery. Living together in sin is one of those newly developed conventions that even Christians are looking upon as normal. It may be normal to the world but it is not normal to God nor should it be normal to followers of Christ. It is adultery and God has commanded us not to commit adultery.

Even homosexuality is being embraced by many who call themselves Christians. Some traditional churches have accepted homosexuality as normal and even accepted practicing homosexuals into the clergy.

Churches that take this position have become puffed up in the sense that they see themselves on the cutting edge of toleration. A large percentage of young evangelicals have embraced homosexuality as normal. They have embraced the world's position on this matter and are proud of their "open minded" stand.

Immorality is rampant in the church and we consider it normal behavior. There is need of repentance. Yet, much of the church is puffed up about it. Not only is there no repentance but many are either proud of their stand or comfortable in the midst of sin and unwilling to deal with it in a godly manner. We want to be popular with the world so we have adopted its ways instead of desiring to please God and adopting His ways.

The Corinthian church did not understand the significance of the gatherings of the church. They were abusing the love feasts by not politely waiting on one another and drinking too much wine (1 Cor. 11:21). Their disrespect for the gatherings of the church and for one another meant that they were not properly discerning the Lord's body, His church. They had forgotten that Christ, the Lamb of God, was sacrificed so that they might spiritually partake of Him and become one body in Christ. Instead, their fleshly behavior had produced factions among them and disregard for the importance of the Lord's Supper.

Many were using the gatherings as an opportunity to show off their ability to speak in tongues (1 Cor. 14). They were disregarding the importance of building up one another and were simply babbling away in their spiritual languages in the public gatherings. Paul made it clear that the purpose of the gatherings was to build one another up spiritually not to display individual gifts meant for personal edification (1 Cor. 14:26).

Today's church in America may not have the specific problems that Corinth had, but it is definitely abusing the gatherings of the church. I have been to churches where the music is so loud that mothers cover the ears of their children and people protect themselves behind the pews. Our meetings are much too large to facilitate open participation which is crucial to the building up of the saints.

We allow one man to dominate the sharing when true koinonia requires sharing on the part of all. The gifts of the Spirit are virtually ignored because the churches have a Sunday agenda that must be adhered to. Paul wrote, "Let all things be done for building up" (1 Cor. 14:26). Everything we do in our gathering should build up the brothers and sisters.

The purpose of mentioning these things is not to condemn the church but to point out its true condition. We don't seem to see and discern our condition in the eyes of the Lord. We are seeing our condition through the prism of the world instead of the word of God.

That brings me to the church in Laodicea. The Lord commissioned John to write a letter to seven churches. The last of these letters is written to Laodicea. In that letter the Lord says, "Because you say, 'I am rich, have become wealthy, and have need of nothing' and do not know that you are wretched, miserable, poor, blind, and naked—I recommend that you buy from Me gold refined in the fire, that you may be rich and white garments, that you may be clothed, that the shame of your nakedness may not be revealed and anoint your eyes with the eye salve, that you may see" (Rev: 3:17,18).

Laodicea was a church that thought it was in excellent spiritual condition. It was self-assured and had become complacent about its true condition. The Lord says, "Because you are lukewarm and neither hot or cold, I will spew you out of My mouth" (v. 16). Obviously this was a church that was neither going forward or backward in progress. It was resting on its laurels and coasting along spiritually.

God's answer for this church is that it would buy from Him "gold refined in the fire." It is the believer who must buy this gold. It does not come without a price. It comes through refining by fire. The Laodiceans had never submitted to the crucible of refining that God uses to purify His people. The gold ore is placed in the crucible and heated to a very hot temperature causing the pure gold to sink to the bottom and the impure dross to rise to the top. By the process of refining, the gold is separated from the impurities.

The church in Laodicea had mingled itself with the world and its false riches and luxurious clothes. God was recommending a way that they could be refined in His purging fire so that they would possess real spiritual riches. They thought they were rich and in need of nothing because they were satisfied with what the world had to offer. God was calling them out of their lukewarm condition into the hot process of refining. Through this process the dross of the world would be separated from their lives and they would come to possess the pure gold of God's presence.

The structured church in America is the Laodicean church today. It thinks it is rich and lacking in nothing. Such thinking leads to a passive attitude. If one thinks that he has already arrived at his destination he surely will pull over and stop traveling. The church in America has pulled over and come to a spiritual stop.

It is self-satisfied and complacent. It is not progressing forward in the faith because it thinks it has everything and need not continue progressing. It preaches a message of wealth and pleasure while avoiding mention of the crucible of God's refining fire. The church is mingled with the world and has been tainted by its impurities. It is time to go to God and purchase "gold refined in fire." It is time to allow God, who is an unquenchable fire, to put us into the crucible for His refining process.

Next the Lord tells the church in Laodicea to buy from Him "white garments, that you may be clothed." The white garments are not the garments of grace that we wear based on our cleansing in the redeeming blood of Christ. These are the white garments of the bride of Christ.

Notice that the Laodiceans were challenged to buy the garments from the Lord. Our justification in Christ has been paid with the price of Christ's blood. We never have to do anything to buy these garments of righteousness. On the other hand, Jesus speaks here of buying these garments from Him. These garments are not given to all Christians but only to those who buy them.

In Revelation 3:4 we see that a few in the church in Sardis were given white garments because "they are worthy." Obviously, these garments were not given to all of the members of the church in Sardis but only the few who had not spoiled their garments.

In Revelation 3:5 we are told that "He who overcomes shall be clothed in white garments." Here only the overcomers are clothed in these garments, not the entire church. The obvious implication is these white garments stand for something unique.

Finally Christ exhorts the church in Laodicea to "…anoint your eyes with eye salve that you may see." Christ was encouraging this church to receive spiritual vision from God so they would be able to see clearly. It was clear that they did not see themselves the way God saw them. They were seeing themselves as "rich, wealthy and in need of nothing" and God saw them as "wretched, miserable, poor, blind and naked."

Paul prayed for the church in Ephesus that they would receive "a spirit of wisdom and revelation… the eyes of your understanding being enlightened" (Eph. 1:17 18). Like the Ephesians, the Laodicea church was in need of God's vision. Their eyes needed to be opened to see the truth about their condition and how it lined up with the purpose of God.

Another passage I want to visit is in the fifth chapter of Ephesians. There Paul wrote, "Christ also loved the church, and gave himself for her, that He might sanctify and cleanse her with the washing of water in the word, that He might present her to himself a glorious church, without stain or wrinkle or any such thing, but that she should be holy and without blemish" (Eph. 5: 25-27).

Christ wants to sanctify His church. The word "sanctify" means to make holy by purification for a purpose. The church is not automatically sanctified as a benefit of justification but must undergo a purification process that separates her from the world and produces in her the likeness of God. Notice the words, "and cleanse her with the washing of water in the word."

This is the process by which the Lord sanctifies His church. He washes her in the cleansing spiritual water contained in His word. The word of Christ cleanses us because it washes away the stains and blemishes of the world. It separates us from the world by purifying our hearts from sin.

Only in this way will the Father have a bride that He can present to His Son at the appointed time. The bride must make herself ready for the wedding. It is interesting that when the wedding comes it is said of the bride that she "...has made herself ready. And to her was granted that she should be clothed in fine linen, clean and white" (Rev. 19:7, 8). There was something she did to prepare herself before God to be clothed with the clean, white, fine linen of the bride.

Paul tells Timothy, "Therefore if anyone cleanses himself from the latter, he will be a vessel for honor, sanctified and useful for the Master, prepared for every good work" (2 Tim. 2:21). Notice that the person "cleanses himself." Through that cleansing he becomes a "vessel of honor, sanctified and useful for the Master."

Many who call themselves Christians remain stained by the world's filthiness because they are unwilling to cleanse themselves. They are unwilling to make themselves ready to be part of the bride of Christ. The structured church in America has watered down the gospel to the point where many believe that if they have made some kind of profession of faith, they are in need of nothing else.

We have adopted a watered-down notion of grace that says, "It doesn't matter how we live as long as we have professed Christ." God has made it clear in His word that if we do not obey Him, we have not believed, for obedience is the evidence of faith.

Now let me take you to the parable of the ten virgins in Matthew chapter 25. Jesus compares the kingdom of heaven to ten virgins who took their lamps and went out to meet the bridegroom. Five of the virgins were wise in that they had purchased plenty of oil for their lamps. The other five were foolish because they did not buy any oil. They thought they would wait until the last minute and buy their oil.

When the bridegroom came the five wise virgins trimmed their lamps and got ready for the bridegroom. The five foolish virgins pleaded with the other five, "Give us some of your oil, for our lamps are going out." But the wise answered, saying, "No, unless there should not be enough for us and you. Go rather to those who sell, and buy for yourselves." While the foolish virgins went to buy oil the "…bridegroom came and the five wise virgins went with him to the wedding, and the door was shut."

Notice that the five foolish virgins were told to "Go rather…and buy for yourselves" (v. 9). This resembles the admonition of the Lord to the church in Laodicea: "Buy from Me gold refined in the fire, that you may be rich" (Rev. 3:18). The gold, white garments and eye salve were to be bought with a price. This implies that Jesus is not referring to the anointing oil that all Christians possess free of charge. This oil must be bought with a price. The price, as with the church in Laodicea, is denial of self. The true follower of Christ must be willing to lose his self-life so that the life of Christ may manifest in his life.

The wise virgins were ready when the bridegroom came because they had taken the time to buy the oil. They were ready for the bridegroom according to His time table. The foolish virgins set their own time table and assumed that He was not coming yet. As a result, they were not ready when He arrived. The oil of God's Spirit was not present in their lives because they had not taken the time to buy it by denying themselves and laying down their lives for Him.

Christians who submit to the time table of God and remain ready at all times, are fulfilling the following admonition of Paul: "There is laid up for me the crown of righteousness, which the Lord, the righteous judge, will give to me on that Day, and not to me only but also to all who loved His appearing." Those who love His appearing receive a crown of righteousness. They are ready for His appearing because they love Him and desire His presence.

Christians who do their own thing without concern for the coming of the bridegroom will not be ready when He comes and obviously will receive no crown. Those who will love His appearing are those who love His presence now. If we do not love being with Him we will not necessarily be excited to see Him at His second coming.

The structured church has rejected the true meaning of discipleship. Sermons are preached on the subject and many words written, but the lives we are living do not bear witness that we are followers of Christ. Many individuals are genuinely following Christ but corporately we have abandoned our testimony. We lack the oneness, love, and spiritual power that bear witness to Him. The world looks on with scorn because they see our hypocrisy.

The Bible makes it clear that there is no middle ground when it comes to being a disciple of Christ. Jesus makes the pathway very clear. He said, "If anyone desires to come after Me, let him deny himself, and take up his cross daily, and follow Me. For whoever desires to save his soul-life will lose it, but whoever loses his soul-life for My sake will save it" (Luke 9:23, 24).

This statement is clear—if a person wishes to follow Christ he must first deny himself. He must take up a cross daily. This means that he must die daily to the things of self and the world.

Jesus talks about two pathways, one broad and one narrow. He said, "Enter by the narrow gate, for the gate is wide and broad that leads to destruction, and there are many who go in by it. For the gate is narrow and difficult is the way which leads to life, and there are few who find it" (Matt. 7:13, 14). These are sobering words. People must realize that following Christ is a serious matter and that it involves a deep commitment. I fear that we have watered down the way of discipleship for the sake of our "have it your way" Americanized Christianity.

When Jesus sent out His disciples on the Great Commission, He did not say, "Go into all the world and convince people to make a decision for Christ." To the contrary, He said, "Go therefore and *make disciples* of all the nations, baptizing them in the name of the Father and the Son and the Holy Spirit, teaching them to keep all things that I have commanded you. And behold, I am with you always even to the end of the age" (Matt. 28:19, 20).

In the Great Commission Jesus charges His disciples to make other disciples. And the way to do that was to baptize them as a symbol of their spiritual death and resurrection and then to teach them to keep the commandments of Jesus. Surely, a true disciple is one who hears from Christ and seeks to obey what He says. He commanded many things during His ministry and He expects His disciples to keep those commandments in the power of the Holy Spirit.

Americanized Christianity preaches all the benefits of Christ without including our responsibility to obey Him. We go through all the motions of spiritual sacrifice but then fail to do what He says. We sing and shout and dance to His honor on Sunday mornings and then live six other days the way we want.

Jesus wants much more from our commitment. He wants our whole heart seven days a week. A spiritual renewal is coming that will give us opportunity to embrace this truth. Get ready to meet God in a very special way. It may be our last chance.

† Chapter 29: The Bride of Christ

When I look at the theme of the last chapter I begin to understand why the Lord assigned certain passages for me to read and study. As I did so, it became obvious to me that Christ would not come back for a church in such a state of impurity.

Like the church in Corinth the church in America is in a state of spiritual carnality. We are like the church in Laodicea, thinking that we are so rich, abounding in possessions, and having no needs and yet we are "wretched, miserable, poor, blind, and naked" (Rev. 3:17). We possess many material things but we lack the spiritual possessions of purity and righteousness.

The promise of the Father is that He would "present her to Himself a glorious church, not having spot or wrinkle or any such thing, but that she should be holy and without blemish" (Eph. 5:27). The garment of the bride is to be without any evidence of the world or sin on it. It is to be perfectly clean and smooth. She is to be holy which means she is set apart for the purpose of God and sanctified by His presence.

The white garments of fine linen of the bride are said to be "the righteous acts of the saints" (Rev. 19:8). The bride is made up of those who have performed righteous acts inspired by the Holy Spirit. We are not talking about the legal righteousness granted to us through the blood of Christ, but the works of righteousness that flow from our relationship with Him.

"In Him we have redemption through His blood, the forgiveness of sins, according to the riches of His grace" (Eph. 1:7). From the point of our redemption we are commissioned to perform the works that He destined for us before the foundation of the world (Eph. 2:10). We will be judged by our works because faith without works is dead (James 2:20).

The believer's judgment is not based on sin but works. God will reward us based on the quality of our works and how they line up with the will of God (1 Cor. 3: 12-15; Eph. 3:10). The righteous deeds of the bride are symbolized by the white garment of fine linen she wears. The words "righteous deeds" imply works done in the will of God, works commissioned and inspired by Him.

The true follower of Christ is not simply devising works based on expediency but is doing what the Lord commands of him. The members of the bride are bondservants of the Lord. They know they are bought with a price. They live accordingly.

The question I asked the Lord was, "Is the bride composed of all Christians or is she a remnant within the church?" In some ways the question may be academic but I firmly believe that a lack of understanding about the church and the bride has produced a passive attitude among Christians. Most evangelicals believe that things will continue as they are and then the rapture will occur, rescuing all born-again believers. There really is no incentive to live a holy life. After all, in their thinking, we all will be raptured regardless of our commitment or spiritual maturity.

Christ is coming back for a church without spot or wrinkle or any such thing, a holy church without blemish (Eph. 5:27). This is not the place to thoroughly make that case. I did that already in my first book *The Eliezer Call* for those who want a comprehensive study of the bride and the church.

For the purpose of these writings what is important is that we understand that the bride is so deeply in love with the Lord that she will do anything for Him and follows Him wherever He goes. I have come to believe that the remnant of Revelation chapter fourteen speaks of the devotion of the bride:

They sang after that a new song before the throne,
before the four living creatures, and the elders, and no
one could learn that song except the hundred and forty-
four thousand who were redeemed from the earth. These are the
ones who were not defiled with women, for they
are virgins. These are the ones who follow the Lamb wherever
He goes. These were redeemed from among
men, firstfruits to God and to the Lamb. And in their mouth was
found no deceit, for they are without blame before the throne of
God (Rev. 14:3-5).

    This remnant, corporate bride is the firstfruits of God's end time harvest. She will be able to sing a song that no one else knew because she will be in tune with the Lord's music of love. She has not defiled herself with other lovers but will have wholly devoted herself to her Bridegroom. Wherever He goes, they follow for they are in love with Him. They have no deceit in their mouths because their hearts have been purified by His presence. Out of the abundance of their hearts their mouths proclaim the glory of their King and speak His word boldly.
    Jesus told many parables. Perhaps the best way to consider the bride of Christ is to think in human terms about a bride preparing for her wedding with her groom. The bride spends hours with her attendants getting beautiful for her groom. Every hair must be in place, every blemish covered, and the gown must be especially beautiful, brilliant, white and spotless.
    Try to imagine a bride who did not take her preparation seriously. Imagine the bride coming forth in everyday clothes stained by the activities of the day. Visualize her hair unkempt and her face plain and blemished. She had not taken the time to prepare herself for her groom. What a disappointment that would be for the groom when she appeared at the head of the aisle.
    The Book of Revelation declares,

Let us be glad and rejoice and give glory to him for the
marriage of the Lamb has come, and His wife has made herself
ready. And it was granted to her to be adorned in fine linen,
clean and white, for the fine linen is the righteous acts of the
saints (Rev. 19:7, 8).

The bride of Christ in this scenario has not simply lived as she wanted as the wedding approached. Her attention was on the day of her wedding and her need to prepare for it. Her attendants were committed to helping her meet that goal. She loved her groom and wanted to please him when she came forth at the wedding.

The truest mark of the bride is that she loves her Groom. She has not given herself to other lovers but is wholly devoted to the One she loves. In this life she has not allowed herself to be conformed to the world but has kept herself pure for her Bridegroom. When He comes she is ready for Him and comes forth in all her glory.

We have a marvelous calling in Christ. The first three chapters of Ephesians reveal the depth and richness of that calling. Paul's writings consistently call us to rise to the challenge of the calling of the bride. For example when Paul begins the fourth chapter of Ephesians he calls us to walk in a way that is worthy of this calling:

> I, therefore, the prisoner of the Lord, beseech you to walk worthy of the calling with which you were called, with all lowliness and gentleness, with longsuffering, bearing with one another in love, endeavoring to keep the unity of the Spirit in the bond of peace.

Paul unveils the calling of God in the first three chapters and then at the beginning of the fourth exhorts his readers to "walk worthy of the calling with which you were called" (4:1). Walking worthy means living in peace, unity and love with others. It means demonstrating humility and gentleness and bearing with the faults of others (4:2, 3). In short it means having the "righteous acts" spoken of in Revelation 19:8. The calling is to prepare for the wedding with Christ. To walk worthy of the calling is the life we live now in obedience to Him.

If you have an ear to hear, you are hearing the calling of Christ to your heart. He is wooing His bride during this engagement period we are in. He has given us His communion meal as an engagement ring reminder of the coming wedding (Luke 22:18, 19). He has given us the Holy Spirit as a guarantee of the inheritance we are to receive as His bride (Eph. 1:14).

Many of our brothers and sisters in Christ have seen this wonderful truth apart from our influence. Our brother and sister Timm and BJ have been sharing this message for many years. They saw this truth when few others saw it. Declaring this message has taken much courage on their part. They spoke the message when it was not popular to do so. Now the message is breaking out and many are beginning to share it.

It falls to us to accept God's gifts from our Bridegroom and prepare ourselves for our future wedding. Let us listen for the loving voice of the Bridegroom. He is calling us to Himself. May we answer the call.

† Chapter 30: The Gathering of the Champions

I'm not sure how I knew but eventually it became clear to me that my time with Christ at the judgment seat had come to an end. Jesus smiled a big smile and began to step down from the mercy seat.

I was sad to see our time come to an end but I knew it was time. All that was left for me was to thank the Lord: "Thank you Lord for the time you have given me here. I have been blessed beyond measure and will miss our times together."

He responded quickly, "This is only the beginning. We have an eternity to spend together in the heavenly realm. You are My son and My brother and I love you."

He came over to me with arms outstretched. As we embraced He said quietly, "Go and be blessed and be a blessing to others."

Then Jesus turned and walked away. I watched Him as He stopped, turned and waved.

Suddenly the cherubim that had carried me to the seat of judgment sprang into action. Their mighty wings began to vibrate according to my movements. When I stood up their mighty wings vibrated and moved to me. When I moved a hand there was a resounding vibration that came from the motion of their immense wings. They were my servants and they prepared to take me to my next station.

Somehow by their power I was lifted up and slowly carried away to a place apparently predetermined. Eventually the mighty angels let me down carefully on a beautiful hillside and disappeared into the celestial sky. As I looked around I noticed I was surrounded by others.

From where I stood among these people I looked across a small valley to see a vast multitude of people surrounded by rejoicing angels. The people in the multitude were all facing someone seated on a throne. Colorful rainbows of light were emanating from the One on the throne.

It was a glorious sight that filled me with indescribable awe. The crowd was praising God in unison as if they had all memorized the lines. They were being guided in their praise by some unseen assistance. The sound of the multitude reminded me of the sound a mighty wave makes when it strikes the beach except it was much louder. This was the most awesome gathering of people I had ever witnessed.

As I observed the amazing multitude and the rainbow radiating from the One on the throne I heard a loud, powerful voice declaring, "Welcome to the gathering of the champions."

At the sound of this announcement I spontaneously fell to my face with all the others who were with me. Something within us responded immediately to the heavenly announcement. Though I didn't know what it meant, somehow I knew that it affected me.

In the middle of the night I awoke thinking that I would resume my conversation with the Lord at the mercy seat only to realize that things were different. Now I was conversing with the Lord in prayer from my bed. It was the same Jesus but the setting was of course different.

"Lord," I prayed, "I heard a voice in heaven saying 'Welcome to the gathering of the champions.' For some reason I was overcome by the announcement and fell to my face. Lord, what is the gathering of the champions?"

In the physical sense things were different now since the conversations at the mercy seat had ended. But I soon realized that spiritually nothing had changed. I could still sit down with Jesus and talk with Him because He was still with me in Spirit. I could no longer see him physically but my spirit sensed His presence and the penetrating nature of His thoughts.

The Lord answered my question just as He had done in heaven but now He spoke to my spiritual ears instead of the physical. I could not see the smile on His face or the twinkle in His eyes but my heart discerned His loving nature.

He quickly replied, "The gathering of the champions is the coming together of My remnant bride. It is the great celebration that follows the marriage of the Lamb and the victory of the last battle. It is the heavenly acknowledgment of My gratitude for their faithfulness. They are the overcomers who defeated all that the world and the enemy threw at them. They are those who endured to the end faithfully fulfilling their calling.

"These are the ones who finished the course set before them. They are the people who loved Me when others walked away. They followed Me wherever I went and faithfully served Me and My saints. They are My precious bride, the realization of My heart's desire."

When Jesus gives an answer there is no second guessing on our part. His answers have a finality to them that dispels any notion of disagreement. In this case it was as if I knew what Jesus was going to say before He said it and was in total agreement with the truth of His answer.

But still there was one more thing I needed to ask. "Lord," I began, "Why was I not part of that multitude that was celebrating before the throne of God? Why were those of us on the hillside separated at a distance from this magnificent event?"

In a very matter-of-fact way the Lord responded, "The fulfillment of your destiny is still in the future. You were joined with others who spoke with me at the mercy seat. My purpose in speaking with you and the others as I did was to inspire you to take the message of My eternal purpose to My people. I have commissioned you to break down the wall of tradition that holds back the revival that is coming."

"But Lord...," I began to question.

Knowing my thoughts the Lord interrupted me and responded to the cry of my heart: "You are wondering about your place in connection with the gathering of the champions. It is not given to Me to tell you of your final reward. Your task is to finish your course without concerns for reward. Love Me. Love My people. Serve them as I have commanded you and your destiny will be fulfilled, your reward secured."

His next words brought a positive sense of finality to my concerns.

With finality in His voice He said, "When your healing is complete take My healing message to the church. Signs and wonders will follow you and others who obey Me. I will be with you to bear witness to the message you proclaim. Do not be concerned about how and when you will present the message. I will be with you always and will empower your words as you proclaim my eternal purpose."

With those comforting words I closed my eyes and went to sleep comfortable in the knowledge that I could speak with My Lord anytime I chose and He would be there to listen and respond. What a joy it is to be His disciple!

✝ Conclusion: How then should we live?

To know Jesus is to change. You cannot truly know Him and remain the same. The more one knows the Lord the more we are compelled to ask the question, "How then should we live?" His presence demands that this question be asked. As we grow in our knowledge of Him we become increasingly aware that He is the Lord and we are to be His servants.

This demands that we seek His will above all and submit our lives to it. In this final chapter I will attempt to pull together the highlights of my conversations with Him.

Seek simple body life with other saints

I begin with this admonition concerning body life because all of the other points seem to be influenced by how we react to it. If we do not have healthy body life we are merely fooling ourselves to think that we are growing spiritually.

Life in the body of Christ is essential to life in Christ. The church is His body, "…the fullness of Him who fills all in all" (Eph. 1:23). The four activities of the early church summarized in Acts 2:42

are not just passing options. They are the essentials of life in the body of Christ.

The apostles' teaching, fellowship, breaking of bread, and prayers. The apostles' teaching is God's word, our spiritual food. The fellowship is like the unity of the systems of the human body working together to assimilate the food into all the parts of the body down to the smallest cell. The breaking of the bread is the Lord's Supper, a way of making Him the guest of honor in our gatherings. Prayers are the way we release the will of heaven into the lives of real people in real situations. Through prayer we remain in communication with the Head, Christ.

Without these essential activities the body of Christ will become sick and will not grow. With them the church will prosper spiritually and growth will be automatic. The saints will be built up and encouraged by the others speaking the truth in love. Passivity will evaporate and active participation will become the norm.

Let me finish this section with a serious admonition. The Book of Hebrews contains a warning that most of us are familiar with:

> Let us consider one another in order to stir up love
> and good works, not forsaking the assembling of ourselves
> together, as is the habit of some, but encouraging one another,
> and so much more as you see the Day approaching.
>
> For if we sin willfully after we have received the knowledge
> of the truth, there no longer remains a sacrifice for sins, but a
> certain fearful expectation of judgment, and fiery indignation
> which will devour the adversaries (Heb. 10: 24-27).

We are familiar with the admonition not to forsake the assembling of ourselves together. Many pastors use this verse to encourage the members to attend church regularly. However, the admonition here means much more than that.

The word translated "assembling" does not mean just coming together in the same place. A breakdown of the word shows that it means a coming together in unity for one purpose. In other words, this passage is encouraging us to make sure that we do not forsake the genuine body life I described earlier.

What follows is a serious warning. The next sentence begins with the connecting word "for" which carries the meaning of "assigning a reason." In other words this passage is saying "let us not forsake body life for the following reason."

Then comes that ominous warning, "For if we sin willfully after we receive the knowledge of the truth, there no longer remains a sacrifice for sins" (v. 26). The author is connecting this warning to the admonition to meet together with the saints. The willful sinning referred to in the passage is apparently the tendency of some to ignore the importance of regular body life and do as they please.

This warning has confounded even the greatest scholars over the years. I don't have space to get into the full ramifications of it. Let us just say at this point that the writer of Hebrews considers assembling with the saints to be of paramount importance. Considering what we have learned about the eternal purpose of God we must surely agree.

Find a context in which you can truly join with other saints as the body of Christ. Commit yourself to God and to the ones who gather with you. Let God lead you in this process. He will not let you down.

Meet with the Lord daily moment by moment

My talks with the Lord have taken away any ambiguity I harbored about prayer. I now see how the Lord wants to meet with us regularly and talk about what is on our hearts and His. The gatherings of the saints are essentially to be sit-down talks with Jesus. He is the guest of honor and should be allowed to lead the conversation of the gathering by the Spirit.

But we don't have to wait until we gather with the saints to talk with Jesus. Each day we can talk to Him throughout the day. After all, He said that He would never leave us or forsake us. He is always there waiting to talk and to listen to our concerns. He genuinely cares about what we think and is the best listener in the universe.

When I was meeting with Jesus in the night visits, I considered it an honor to be there with Him. We must understand the honor we have of living in fellowship with the Master, who is both our brother and our King.

He is with us through the Holy Spirit and He has promised that the Spirit will lead us into all truth. Jesus said of the Holy Spirit, "He will glorify Me, for He will take of what is mine and declare it to you. All things that the Father has are mine. Therefore I said that He will take of mine and declare it to you" (John 16:14, 15).

This means that the Holy Spirit is bringing to us what belongs to Jesus. As the Holy Spirit speaks He is presenting to us the things that belong to Jesus. Jesus possesses all that belongs to the Father. All that He does and says glorifies the Lord.

All of this makes talking with Jesus a special experience. All of the riches of the Father are available to us through prayer. His healing power, and His saving presence become real to us as we meet with Him. He changed the lives of so many people during His earthly ministry simply by having a conversation with them.

The woman at the well, Lazarus and his family, Matthew and his friends, Zacchaeus, the apostles and many others experienced changed lives as a result of sitting down with Jesus and talking with Him. His words are liberating.

Take up your cross daily

Jesus said, "If anyone will come after Me, let him deny himself, and take up his cross daily, and follow Me" (Luke 9:23). To take up a cross is to go to one's death. Each day we must be willing to die to self in order to follow Christ. It is impossible to truly follow Him if our fallen, selfish soul is insisting on its own way. It must die daily so we can follow Christ to where He is leading.

Life in Christ begins with self denial. Most religions, including organized Christianity, elevate the soul and emphasize self, but Christ said that the soul must die in order for us be free to follow Him. If we call Him Lord we must be willing to allow Him to be Lord of our lives. Many call Him Lord but do not do what He says (Luke 6:46).

John puts it even more bluntly: "He who says, 'I know Him,' and does not keep His commandments, is a liar, and the truth is not in him" (1 John 2:4). Those words are in stark contrast to the permissive attitude much of the church has at this time. Those who say they know Christ but live their lives the way they want to, are lying both to themselves and to others. His presence in us will change us gradually into His image.

Paul encourages us to "walk worthy of the calling with which you were called" (Eph. 4:1). The next two verses in this passage speak of lowliness, gentleness, longsuffering, bearing with one another in love, and keeping the unity of the Spirit with our fellow Christians. To walk worthy means to have a life with other people that reflects the Christ who dwells within us.

This is where bearing the cross comes in. If we are a hermit living in a cave somewhere there is little need of bearing the cross. But when we are living in relationship with others there are many occasions for our self to be denied for the sake of others. As we lay down our own lives for the sake of Christ and His people, the church grows and everyone is blessed. The problem is that many Christians are living like hermits by living in isolation from others.

Our commandment is to love one another (1 John 2:8-10). Love results in you preferring others over yourself. Putting others first is the most obvious evidence of love. Self denial is the outcome of love. Jesus bore His cross because He loves us. Now we are asked to bear our cross because we love Him and His people.

Look beyond the wall of tradition that holds back revival

As I said earlier Christ's calling on my life is to help tear down the wall of tradition that holds back the new wineskin that God has prepared for His church. Tradition is living our lives in yesterday. Religious people tend to desire the comfort of tradition because it allows them to relax and not be concerned about the new challenges that always come.

Revival is thwarted by those who insist that yesterday's understanding trumps the new thing the Lord wants to usher in. Revival cannot come until people allow the wall of tradition to be torn down so they can move forward into the new experience God is bringing.

Your challenge is to look beyond the wall of tradition to the new thing God has prepared. As you do so God's vision will be birthed in your heart. You will find yourself unsatisfied with the stale manna you have gathered but desiring the fresh new provisions of God.

God wishes to pour out new wine into His people but He must have a new wineskin that will contain it. New wine is still expanding due to fermentation and it will burst the old dried up leather wineskin. The old, stiff wineskin must be discarded and replaced with a fresh, stretchable one that will expand when the new wine is poured.

God help us all to look beyond the walls of tradition to the new provision of God. Some of us are called to tear down that wall but all of us are encouraged to receive God's revelation so we can see beyond the wall into the freedom of God's next move. Jesus is outside of the walls of religion and if we desire to meet with Him we too must go outside the camp bearing His reproach (Heb. 13:13, 14).

Love the Lord as your Bridegroom

Some people get offended when we suggest that the bride is a remnant within the church. Many want to be included in the bride without loving the Bridegroom. I encourage all followers of Christ to seek to love Him as a bride loves her groom. That means forsaking all other lovers for Him alone. It means abandoning the offerings of the world to be devoted to Him. The bottom line is that it means putting Him first in all things.

Being part of His bride also means loving His people. We cannot say we love Him while we fail to love His children. After all, the bride is corporate, made up of many saints. It follows, then, that if love prefers others, a unified, loving, caring church will arise when saints simply love one another. It can actually be said that to love the Bridegroom produces the bride because love for Him is also expressed in love toward the other members of His bride.

The Song of Solomon may be interpreted as a love story depicting the love of Christ and His bride for one another. As their love grows in the Song the bride declares, "I am my beloved's, and his desire is toward me" (7:10). Oh that we would be able to declare in truth, "I am my beloved's," that we are wholly His and belong to no other. His desire has always been toward us for He destined us as His chosen one. It is time for us to fall in love with our Bridegroom and prepare ourselves for the approaching wedding.

Live free of sin and its effects

When I teach on this subject some people think I am saying that we must live in sinless perfection. To the contrary, it is possible to live free of sin and its devastating effects through confession and forgiveness, without resorting to the notion of sinless perfection.

John wrote, "If we confess our sins, He is faithful and just to forgive us our sins and to cleanse us from all unrighteousness" (1 John 1:9). The word translated confess in this verse carries the idea of assenting or agreeing with someone else. It also implies entering into covenant with another person. If we are in covenant with God we are agreeing with His assessment of our sins. Confessing is not just saying words but having a genuine, from the heart, agreement with God concerning our sins.

The apostle also wrote, "But if we walk in the light as He is in the light, we have fellowship with one another, and the blood of Jesus Christ His Son cleanses us from all sin" (1 John 1:7). Walking in the light means walking with Jesus, for He is the light and in Him there is no darkness. As we walk with Him in the light we are able to have fellowship with one another because all the hindrances to fellowship are destroyed in the light of His presence.

Sin cannot exist in the light of His presence. The darkness of sin will be revealed in stark contrast to the Light. When we see it revealed we will confess it and He will forgive us and cleanse us from the unrighteousness and its effects. John says, "He is faithful and just to forgive us." He never fails to do His part for His blood secured our justification and redemption.

Jesus made it very clear to me in my talks with Him that it is a mockery of the cross to fail to forgive ourselves or to assume that He has not forgiven us. He is faithful. He proved that when He went to the cross. He does His part well. Now it falls to us to do our part in walking in His light through fellowship with Him and continuous confession and cleansing.

One of the most devastating sins is unforgiveness. Through unforgiveness a person tries to replace God by becoming another person's judge.

Jesus tells a parable that emphasizes this truth. In the parable a servant owes his master a large amount of money. When he asks for compassion his master forgives him the debt. Later when one of his fellow servants came to him asking for compassion for a debt the wicked servant had him thrown into jail. When the master found out about it he had the unforgiving servant thrown into prison with the torturers until he paid his debt.

Jesus explains the significance of the parable: "So My heavenly Father will also do to you if each of you, from his heart, does not forgive his brother his offences" (Matt. 18:35). Jesus repeats this thought after the Lord's prayer, "But if you do not forgive men their sins neither will your Father forgive your sins" (Matt. 6:15).

Unforgiving people are living in serious error and according to these statements will not receive forgiveness from God for their sins.

Unforgiveness is a breeding ground in the heart for disobedience. The church can never form or exist where people are unwilling to forgive.

I have heard grown people say such things as, "I'm not coming to the church gathering if so and so is there." Such people set themselves up as judge and jury regarding the sins of others. They keep the body of Christ in a state of immaturity and their own lives in a shambles. They judge others but will not judge themselves that truth may prevail.

I realize that this is a tough message and it will offend many Christians. I am not trying to cause offense but this is a serious message that is avoided by most preachers. The words of Jesus and Paul are stronger than mine and they must be heeded.

To find victory over sin you must also forgive yourself as well. It is a mockery of the cross to condemn yourself when Christ has forgiven you based on the cross. His death has secured our justification from sin and His life in us secures cleansing from unrighteousness. We need to trust the work of the cross and the Christ who died there.

Freedom from the power of sin is possible if we learn to confess our sins and live in the freedom of His forgiveness and the comfort of His cleansing power.

Be in the world but not of it

Satan is the god of this world system. He has developed it from the beginning for his own sinister plan. The world is the means by which the enemy presents to people what he stands for and what he has to offer. Most people buy into his offerings. Even many Christians have been duped by his deceptive tactics.

Paul exhorts us with these well-known words: "And do not be conformed to this world, but be transformed to the renewing of your mind, that you may prove what is that good and acceptable and complete will of God" (Rom. 12:2). We must understand that it is inevitable we will change in one way or another. We will either gradually conform to the world and thus be changed by Satan's evil strategy, or we will be transformed to the renewing of our minds by the influence of the Holy Spirit.

With a renewed mind we are able to prove in our own hearts the will of God. The world will change us from the outside but leave our mind unrenewed. Such people are confused and without direction in their lives because they cannot discern God's will. They flounder and struggle for meaning in life only to be let down by Satan's futile system.

Some Christians think that there are no commandments in the New Testament because of God's grace. To the contrary, the Lord commands many things through the New Testament writers. The apostle John says, "Do not love the world or the things in the world. If anyone loves the world, the love of the Father is not in him" (1 John 2:15). This is not only a command concerning the world but it also contains a serious warning that if we love the world we do not possess the love of the Father.

The world is the antithesis of the Father's will. If we love it then we obviously have chosen to turn our back on God. Christians are called out of the world to be a sanctified, set apart, special, people committed only to their God.

We must be in the world in order to be ambassadors for Jesus Christ to the people, but we are not to be part of it. As Peter says we are "sojourners and pilgrims" (1 Peter 2:11) not permanent residents of the world. We are merely passing through as representatives of Jesus Christ.

Prepare for the collapse of America

This book would not be complete without a warning about the future collapse of this once great country. The Lord spoke very clearly to me that America will experience a major financial, social and political collapse.

He did not give me any timetable for this but I feel certain that it will come during my lifetime. I agree with others who are saying that our present economic troubles are not the collapse the Lord spoke of. We will survive the current recession but a future collapse is certain.

Now the question is "How do we prepare for this collapse?" Do we store up food and water? Do we sell everything and settle all debts?

All of the other things I have shared in this concluding chapter form the answer to this question. If we talk to the Lord and deny ourselves daily while maintaining healthy body life, He will communicate to us the steps to be taken.

The answer lies not in human pragmatism and cleverness but in the Holy Spirit. As we listen to Him and are led by the Spirit we will be guided step by step. It is entirely possible that the Lord may encourage many to get out of debt, move to other areas of the country, or begin storing nonperishable items. Some may even be led to develop gardens or raise livestock to supplement their food supply. We need to be open to the Lord, listening intently for His guidelines in the coming days.

On the other hand we serve a supernatural God who does not need natural things for His answers. Jesus fed the multitude with two fish and five loves of bread. He caused money to materialize in the mouth of a fish. He multiplied the fish in the nets of the disciples. He healed the sick and raised the dead. This is the Lord we serve. In times of need He will not let us down. We do not depend on the financial system but on our miracle-working God.

Prayer is essential to hearing from God. When the Lord walked away from our meetings I was encouraged to find that I could still meet with Him and talk with Him in prayer. Every believer can come "…with confidence to the throne of grace, that we may receive mercy and obtain grace to help in time of need" (Heb. 4:16). We are entering a serious time of need and it is crucial that we spend much time at His throne in prayer so His grace and mercy can meet our needs and clarify our path.

The words of the well-known proverb are especially helpful at this time: "Trust in the Lord with all your heart and lean not on your own understanding. Know Him in all your ways and He will straighten your paths" (Prov. 3:5, 6).

The key in this passage is to know Him. The traditional translation is rendered "acknowledge" but the Hebrew word means to know Him, or to have a relationship with Him. As we travel down life's pathways, He is our travel companion and we consult Him concerning all turns in the path. He straightens our paths by sharing His wisdom which helps to eliminate diversions. He directs our travel on the pathway as we know Him and let Him lead us.

It is crucial, as the proverb encourages, to trust the Lord with all our heart. The psalmist says, "I will say of the Lord, 'He is my refuge and my fortress; my God in Him I will trust'" (Ps. 91:2). In times of trouble we declare our trust in God. We lean on His everlasting arms. He will never let us down.

Becoming prepared for the approaching collapse has its answer in God. Do not lean on your own understanding or that of others. Get to know Him closely and listen to the voice of the Holy Spirit. If you lean on Him He will uphold you and keep you from falling.

Stay close to God and to His people. That is the core message of this book. Open to the revelation of His eternal purpose and let it change your life according to His will. Cease from all your fleshly work and rest in Him. Go and follow Him. Follow Him where He leads. Let Him be Lord. God bless you all.

A Final Word

I have been privileged to meet with Jesus under the most extraordinary circumstances. What I have experienced has changed my life. I hope that my account of these visits will serve to encourage other saints to come boldly to the throne of grace to meet Jesus.

I hope that you will come to see Jesus as your Friend and brother as well as your King and Lord. We serve a King who has died to make His subjects His brothers, family members in His majestic kingdom. He has made us kings and priests in that kingdom. He does not rule us as religious subjects but woos us as precious members of His corporate bride.

I am quite aware that this book is a hard message in places. This is because the message of Christ is absolute, not vacillating and compromised like much of religion. He is God. His words are either "yes, yes" or "no, no." His word, recorded in scripture, is not subject to opinion or the changing views of men. He does not speak and then allow us to stretch His words into the meaning we want. His words are simple and direct.

The doctrines that develop out of the words of Jesus are not merely for our intellectual stimulation but are meant to guide our lives. They are the ideas of God given to us to bring us joy and happiness. When He commands something He is not making a suggestion but is mandating behavior on our part. He does so because He loves us and wants His best for us.

We tend to think that God will water down His truth to suit our whimsical attitude or the toleration message of modern religion. Jesus speaks only truth. He cares about what we think but He never adjusts His truth based on the religious winds that blow. We must come to see this absolute nature of the Lord or we will never be able to fully embrace His message to mankind and His church.

And now I must turn my attention to the assignment He has given me. He has commissioned me to work with others to bring down the wall of tradition that holds back God's renewal.

Many of you will be called to the same commission. Regardless of your call, I pray that you will obey Him and courageously go where He calls you. May we hear from our God and have the courage to fulfill His commission for our lives.

This narrative is about Him. It is an eye opening account that reminds us of the loving, tender nature of our Savior. We are reminded that our sins are under His blood because of His supreme sacrifice. We are drawn to Him as an espoused bride is drawn to her Groom. He is our Lord, Savior, Master, King, Brother, and Husband. All that He has done and all that He will do in the future is aimed at blessing us with His best. Everything He does seeks to help His bride prepare for the grand heavenly wedding. He loves us all with perfect love. He loves you enough to sit down with you and talk any time you desire.

God bless all of you as you meet with Him face to face and discover His amazing grace.

PS: I recently received my last chemo-therapy treatment. Though I am feeling the nausea and weakness that follow the treatments, I am overjoyed to know that Jesus has promised me victory over this challenge. Join with me in celebrating this great victory in the Lord. Thanks to all who have suffered with me. Now is the time to rejoice. "Great is the Lord, and greatly to be praised."

PSS: I received the results of a PET/CT scan recently. The results showed no cancer in my system. I am continuing to grow stronger each day and look forward to a full recovery. Keep praying that the enemy's scare tactics will fail and God's promise of victory will be embraced. Praise our God!

Made in the USA
Charleston, SC
04 March 2010